THE CHILD

IN THE CHURCH

THE CHILD

IN THE CHURCH

By
Maria Montessori and others

Edited by E.M. Standing

HILLSIDE EDUCATION

Cover and interior book design by Mary Jo Loboda with thanks to MCCI (Montessori Catechetical and Cultural Institute)

Cover image: *Madonna della seggiola* (Madonna of the Chair), by Raphael, courtesy of Wikimedia

ISBN: 978-0-9991706-1-8

Hillside Education, 2017
475 Bidwell Hill Road
Lake Ariel, PA 18436
www.hillsideeducation.com

CONTENTS

MONTESSORI AND POPE ST. JOHN XXIII

The late Pope John, when he was Patriarch of Venice, was pleased to celebrate Holy Mass for the participants of the Fourth National Montessori Conference. At the end of the ceremony, he addressed a particularly cordial greeting to those attending.

In a brief discourse he stressed the value of Montessori education, inspired by respect and love for the child, and mentioned the fundamental principles of the method. He also recalled his meeting with Doctor Montessori when he was Apostolic Nuncio at Paris.

Pope John said: "It is possible to see a clear analogy between the mission of the Shepherd in the Church and that of the prudent and generous educator in the Montessori method, who with tenderness, with love and with a wise evaluation of gifts, knows how to discover and bring to light the most hidden virtues and capacities of the child."

FROM THE VITA DELL' INFANZIA

Preface

This book is made possible through collaboration with the Montessori Catechetical and Cultural Institute (MCCI). MCCI was founded in 2002 to facilitate the opening of Montessori Atria beginning with the Atrium at St. Catherine of Siena Catholic Church in Great Falls, Virginia, and to sponsor training programs to prepare catechists for certification in the Montessori-based Catechesis of the Good Shepherd. We are proud to re-release this 1965 edition of E.M. Standing's edited work so that a new generation of parents and catechists will be able to help foster the child's relationship with God. For more information, visit us online at www.montessori-mcci.org.

Editor's Foreword

Thirty years have passed since the first edition of this book appeared. During that interval world history has unfolded itself with astounding rapidity. We have lived through a Second World War, now being followed by the Cold War, during which a bewildered humanity carries on from day to day under the imminent threat of an apocalyptic catastrophe.

It is quite possible that historians of the future—looking back to this period through a perspective of centuries—may note that it was an epoch remarkable for two tremendously important discoveries, both relating to the release of energies hitherto unknown and unimplemented. One was the discovery and release of the titanic forces locked up in the atom; the other, the beneficial release of hitherto unsuspected energies, intellectual and spiritual, in the souls of children.

From the point of view of the history of the Church the most striking event in those years is the Ecumenical Council with all that it implies in the present and the future. From the point of view of our immediate task—this second and much enlarged edition of *The Child in the Church*—the most significant happening was the death of Madame Montessori at the age of 82 years on May 12, 1952. Happily her work and her influence in the sphere of education did not die with her. In fact, she left behind her a movement more dynamic, more extended—and extending—than at any previous time in her long career. Official and unofficial training centers for Montessori teachers exist in most of the capitals of Europe—also in India and Ceylon—while Montessori schools are found, and new ones keep cropping up, in almost every part of the world.

In the United States, after a long period of quiescence, there has been a remarkable renaissance of Montessori activity. The Montessori principles collectively form a dynamic energy which continues to operate quite independently of the genius who discovered them. During the past half century, since Montessori began her work in 1907, this "leaven" has gone on working in ever-widening spheres; first, geographically, that is to say in more and more countries; and secondly, psychologically, in the application of her principles to more advanced epochs in human development and to an ever-increasing variety of subjects, including religion.

Inside the Catholic Church important changes have been taking place with regard to methods of teaching religion. The *Baltimore Catechism* with its "Parrot System" has been more and more criticized and more and more felt to be inadequate. Many experiments have been and are still being made to find a better method, but, as yet, there seems to be no general consensus as to what is the best substitute. Meanwhile, with the upsurge of a neo-paganism which attacks the Church ever more fiercely and in ever new forms, the need for a vital method of religious training has become ever more urgent.

It is our conviction that the method discovered by Doctor Montessori has laid down the general lines along which this problem can best be solved. And we say this not simply because Montessori was a Catholic, but because there exists, by its very nature, a profound affinity between the Montessori Method and the psychological approach used by the Church in her liturgy. Montessori herself admitted to the present writer on more than one occasion that in the working out of her own educational ideas she learned much from what she called the "pedagogical method" of the Church. Furthermore, she put on record that—as one of the results of her experiments, particularly in Barcelona—her own method could only find its fullest expression when applied to the teaching of the Catholic faith. In fact, she was convinced that this new method was, by a peculiar and providential concatenation of circumstances, placed in her hands for the advancement of the kingdom of God through its application to teaching the truths of the Catholic faith. All her life, too, she entertained the idea that the formation of a new religious order might be the most appropriate means for the carrying out of her work—a point to which we shall return later.

We have thought it appropriate in this second edition to say something about Montessori as a Catholic. In this connection we should like to express our deep gratitude to Signorine Maccheroni for the valuable firsthand information which she has provided. "Macch," as her friends call her, is the only surviving disciple of Montessori who was there from the very beginning and was one of the first to devote her life, with its many brilliant talents, to the *Dottoresa's* work.

Since the first edition of this book in 1929, a great deal of research has been going on quietly and unobtrusively in a number of Montessori schools in different countries, on the application of Montessori principles to the teaching of religion. We are fortunate in being able to include in this volume descriptions and illustrations of some of this interesting and original work. Among those who have contributed in this manner, we would like to express our gratitude to the Reverend Mother Isabel Eugenie, who was for many years an intimate friend of Doctor Montessori. It was through her influence that Montessori gave a course of lectures on the teaching of religion at the Assumption College in London in 1936, from which we have drawn copiously in the following pages. We are grateful also to the Reverend Sister Stephanie, O.S.F., and her staff for photographs of children working with materials which they have devised. No less are we grateful to the Marchesa Sofia Cavalletti for her valuable outline of the work that goes on in her Maria Montessori School of Religious Teaching, in via degli Orsini 34 in Rome, and also for illustrations of that work. Nor can we omit to thank Monsieur and Madame Lanternier for the fascinating and original example of the liturgical work which they have been carrying on at the Montessori Center in Rennes, France.

It is beyond question that the complete application of Montessori's principles to the teaching of religion is something which still belongs to the future. Its fulfillment will require the loving and disciplined labor of many collaborators in a field which still contains many areas of virgin soil. We hope that some readers will devote themselves to this important task.

The publication of this book has been held up a number of times owing to ill health and other causes. Mr. Donald Demarest, my friend and editor, has shown himself as patient on these occasions as he has been always helpful with his valuable advice and encouragement.

We are indebted to Catechetical Guild and its founder, Rev. Louis A. Gales, for publishing *The Child in the Church*. Among other good things that grew out of the Guild, now in its 33rd year, is the *Catholic Digest* as well as a wealth of audio-visual materials which are quite Montessorian.

In the first edition of this book there was a chapter on the Principles of the Montessori Method. In view of the pressure of new materials this has been omitted in the second edition. Those who wish to acquaint themselves with a general outline of Montessori's educational ideas are referred to *The Montessori Method—A Revolution in Education* (Academy Library Guild) by the present writer.

It has been found convenient to divide this second edition of *The Child in the Church* into three sections: the first by Montessori; the second by the editor and others; while the third is of a practical nature being concerned with putting into practice the principles discussed in parts one and two.

Last but not least I would like to put on record my deep gratitude to the Sisters of Providence—in particular to the Reverend Mother Judith, Provincial, and to the Reverend Sister Margaret Jane, Superior —for their genial and generous hospitality which has enabled me to devote my energies entirely to Montessori work in a "Home" which has become a real home to me.

E. MORTIMER STANDING

Mount St. Vincents,
4831-35th Ave., S.W.,
Seattle 26,
Washington, U.S.A.
June, 1965

PART ONE

CHAPTER ONE

GOD AND THE CHILD

When a great evolution occurs it has inner premonitory signs, because all progress originates within some human mind. In fact, an important discovery is never an isolated one. It occurs simultaneously in several places, through different people who have nothing in common. When we say "there are ideas floating in the air," we really mean that new forms or ideas or feelings have taken shape in the minds of men, as if by a spontaneous energy, brought to focus with the passing of time by a phenomenon of collective growth.

It is interesting to observe that in this century peculiar phenomena have occurred in children's souls. It seems that children have really succeeded in revealing themselves in all the splendor of their spiritual manifestations.

In the beginning of this century, the phenomenon of normalization took place in our schools. By this we mean that a group of about forty little children changed their character, almost their nature, revealing profound characteristics in the child's soul which had previously remained unknown. The little children showed us the interior laws for the formation of man, which have given rise to a method of education that has spread throughout the world among every race. The manifestations of these children brought people in pilgrimage from across oceans and continents to this "Children's Mecca" in Rome.

This group of children influenced adults of all social conditions so deeply that many of them felt that a better world was at hand. They began talking (around 1907) about "the discovery of the human soul," about "miracles," about "conversions" in children, about the "New Children," and finally about visions of the kingdom of heaven. People of every religious and political party, of every social class, became greatly interested in it.

But the most interesting thing about it was to find out why people with ideas and sentiments so different or even so contradictory—as for example, monarchists and communists, Catholics, Jews and Buddhists —were so intensely interested in the children's manifestations, and what it was they discovered in the things the children were doing that seemed so important in relation to their own convictions. Well, this was the reason: everyone was finding something there that was wanting in achievement of their own ideals, and saw in these manifestations the necessary help toward the triumph of their own principles. That is to say, every section of the adult world, no matter to what party, what religious faith or ideal it belonged—even those whose beliefs and ideals had nothing in common—recognized in the child the necessary element for its own triumph. Unfortunately the profound significance of these marvelous manifestations was not fully realized; and too little were they considered as the result of the child's own powers, given him by the Creator.

God Created The Child More Admirable Than We Think

These prodigious manifestations of the child's soul were considered to be the result of an educational method. Many thought that these children developed in this manner because they were educated in a special way. The success of this change in the children was attributed to the pedagogic abilities of the adults, who usually claim the favorable development of children as their own educational influence, just as they blame the lack of good will on the children's part on the children's own bad intentions.

And so, instead of research into the juvenile soul, its own powers and the goal toward which it is internally directed by its unwarped nature, there developed a series of discussions, arid and useless, on the method. But it was not the method which had produced those marvelous manifestations. It was rather the surprising phenomena manifested in a life free from the influence of any special method which led to the creation of our method or, at least, to its more perfect development.

Many thought, instead, that this manner of helping the child through a method was like a newly discovered talisman which could bring about the most miraculous results. And they set about making experiments to see if it were not possible to discover an even more talismanic method which would obtain even more precious results. But only too little did they realize that the further perfecting of the educational system would depend strictly on a more complete discovery of the various impulses to growth in the child, during the successive phases of his development, and on finding out those conditions under which this urge to development would find its best unfolding. And so we found ourselves facing the danger that children would be subjected to all sorts of experiments; and instead of revealing more clearly their true nature, would be impeded in their natural manifestations.

Educationists ought rather to have investigated the wonderful powers of divine creation in the child's soul. It was the nature of the child himself that was worthy of their admiration, rather than a method which was merely an adaptation to those inner, divine "directives" which govern the natural course of development.

Now, as we said above, discoveries are never made by one person only. It was not only in the year 1907 that the "new children" appeared on the earth. History tells us about similar "apparitions" which, however fleeting, have remained in the memory of posterity, almost like unreal descriptions. In the eighteenth and nineteenth centuries, the impressive spectacle of children's souls happy at work, exalted in the enthusiasm of their knowledge, was also seen, but it vanished like a vision seen out of its time, and which, for this reason, could not be produced again.

Pestalozzi also witnessed the extraordinary progress of his pupils for which he, the teacher, was not responsible. The reason why so many people consider this prodigious progress as the result of Pestalozzi's educational ability comes from the fact that they are still more skeptical when confronted with discoveries which are made in the field of the child's soul, than in any other field. It is unpleasant for them to admit that the child's soul was, until then, unknown to them. They cannot admit that the child was concealing, as if behind a mask, his elevated nature, his formidable energies and rich initiative; nor can they admit the statement that it was a psychological ignorance on the part of the educator which was to be blamed for this state of affairs. They prefer to attribute to the adult's competence such successes in the children. But Pestalozzi's own words compel us to give the children all the credit. Here is how Pestalozzi disclaims that he had anything to do with the marvelous manifestations he observed:

"Those who attended my lessons were amazed by the

result In fact it was like a flash of lightning which dazzles and disappears. I myself did not understand the meaning of my work. It was the result of an idea of which I had no clear understanding."

Evidently Pestalozzi had unconsciously given his pupils the help *which enabled them to act by themselves;* and he witnessed with amazement results disproportionate to and independent of his action. This is what he said: "Prodigious experiment! Even a discerning man would not have dared to do it—and I, myself, would not have dared either—if by pure luck I had not been blind. I do not know, I cannot even begin to understand how it succeeded. The feeling of fatigue which reigns in every school disappeared as if by magic from my school. The pupils had the will to work, and the capacity. They were persevering, successful, full of joy, and never oppressed by their studies. One would have said they belonged to another race."

Interesting also are the following words: "They (the children) exalt God's work in the child. Men do not know what God does for them. They do not attach any importance to nature's influence on education. On the other hand, they make a great show of all the trifles that THEY superimpose upon this all powerful action, as if everything depended on their own ability. I noticed the same thing in myself when I wished to claim unduly for myself the running of a machine already wound up and working of its own accord." With these words Pestalozzi makes it clear that the extraordinary success of his school was not so much due to his educational ability as to the marvelous impulse to development that God has created in the child's soul and to which Pestalozzi was giving every opportunity for expansion.

About a century later, Tolstoi had, in his school at Isnaia Poliana, little peasant children who came to him from their miserable hovels where everyone was illiterate, and yet he saw them all lit up by the flame of interest at the reading of history and biblical stories, with a constancy and enthusiasm which astonished him. It was after this experience that Tolstoi declared that the most valuable thing in the world is linked with the child's soul.

And how many, also today in our times, have begun to be convinced of this? Is it not perhaps in the souls of the young that Rabindranath Tagore puts his trust when he leads these young people to the banks of the sacred river, the Ganges, and expects some divine manifestation to emanate from their souls?

God Gave the Child a Nature of His Own

There are some of those who think that the child's only value for humanity lies in the fact that he will some day be an adult. In this way they detract from the true value of childhood by shifting it only into the future. This cannot be justified. The child is a human entity having importance in himself; he is not just a transition on the way to adulthood. We ought not to consider the child and the adult merely as successive phases in the individual's life. *We ought rather to look upon them as two different forms of human life, going on at the same time, and exerting upon one another a reciprocal influence.* The child and the adult are in fact two different and separate parts of humanity which should interpenetrate and work together in the harmony of mutual aid.

Therefore, not only must the adult aid the child, but the child must also aid the adult. The first proposition is accepted by all as a self-evident truth; but not everyone realizes that the child is a wonderfully precious aid to the adult, and that he can, and should—in accordance with the will of God—

exercise a formative influence on the adult world. Such a statement tends to be regarded with a certain degree of skepticism as a modern notion, but a calm meditation on this idea will lead to its acceptance.

That the child should have a nature quite different from the adult would not seem to require further proof; but what *is* necessary to point out is that this difference is much deeper than most people think. From the physical standpoint, infancy is a constant state of growth and transformation; the dynamics of inner life constantly spur the child toward new conquests, quantitative and qualitative; whereas the adult is rather spurred on to preserve what he has acquired. The old concept that the germ cell already contains in minute dimensions what the adult has in enlarged dimensions— so that growth would mean just increased dimensions— has been definitely abandoned. Man's growth is not just an increase; it is rather a constant metamorphosis, even in physical proportions. If, for example, the proportion between the torso and the head remained that of the newborn, we would all be monstrous adults. The profound difference between adult and child reveals itself also in the fact that children need food, rest and movement of an altogether different kind, and keep changing accordingly.

This characteristic difference is seen not only in the physical field, but also in the psychic one. The child feels, thinks and aspires in an entirely different manner from adults. He interprets and observes all things in his own special way. Even what happens to him is experienced differently. Hence, the children's reactions are so profoundly different from those of the adult's that the adults are sometimes at a loss how to understand their children's reactions. The child requires his own means and his own method in order to develop. An appropriate time, rhythm and duration characterize his every activity. The forms in which his psychic life manifests itself, his needs and his ability to express himself, do not correspond with those of the adult.

While the adult mainly directs his actions in accordance with conventions, the child is irresistibly spurred on by inner impulses. Also the interests of the child are not the same as those of the adult. Indeed they differ so much from them that often this difference leads to tensions and conflicts. A child, for instance, out for a walk with his mother is attracted by objects which to her have no importance whatever. He will fling himself upon a shining object which the adult considers worthless—mere rubbish to be thrown away. This great difference in the psychic field between the adult and the child is so evident that no one would deny it. On the contrary it is a phenomenon universally recognized and valued.

Here we want only to show that the presence of this infant life, so deeply different from the adult life, exerts a profound influence just because of its radically opposite character. Let us imagine for a while that the world consisted only of adults, because man was born already developed and mature; and because of this could dispense with parents. The most basic community, the family, which of all natural communities exerts a deeper and more lasting influence on the spirit of man, and which sets itself up both by means of, and because of the child with his many needs, would then have no more reason to exist. Not only would this profoundly change our manner of life, but it would also change man himself. The tender, intimate, affectionate, reverent, adaptable and familiar sentiments of the heart, which unfold through the many years of relationship between child and parents, would be replaced by entirely different characteristics. Not only would the children of men be different but also the parents themselves.

It is just through his condition of being a son that the child is able to change, for the good, the adults around him. Is not the life of self forgetfulness and sacrificing love which centers around the child and the satisfaction of his needs something which is at once noble, uplifting and character-building? The child is indeed not conscious of his formative influence on the adults, and therefore does not consider himself as an apostle. But what is proper to the child—his natural innocence, his affection, his self-abandon, his defenseless condition and his touching appeal for help, his timorous cry when he finds himself alone or in danger—all of these marvelously move the human heart.

The child can change the hearts of men; in the midst of children their hardness disappears. The child can annihilate selfishness and awaken the spirit of sacrifice. This happens every time a child is born in a family. Often the parents are afraid before the coming of the child; but when he is born and placed in his mother's arms, and when the father, full of admiration, contemplates the fruit of his love, then arises in their hearts emotions of tenderness and the impulse to affectionate care. The love, which then begins, is like a revelation of the moral greatness of which man is capable when his child obliges him to feel as a father. Then his own resources become those of the child. All the powers of which he is capable are directed toward the defense and protection of his children. He works for them and is willing to sacrifice everything to preserve them. In this way does God move and form the adult through the child.

This is the significance of the child in the life of the adult. And this meaning will be even more significant when the adult's spirit of sacrifice is directed not only toward preserving the physical life and health of the child, but also toward the development of what is spiritual and divine in his soul. Because of what the child stands for and his needs we may regard him as a great external grace which enters the family, in which he fulfills the apostolate of the child.

The Influence Which the Child Has Upon the Life of Adults Has Been Too Small

The child exercises the functional direction of his own life for too short a period and in a too limited sphere. As long as his little body is in a state of complete helplessness the adult is all attention and responds to his every real need—and, not infrequently, to those that are not real needs. To correspond and conform to these physical needs is considered as a simple duty, because these are objective needs, based on the child's right to have a healthy physical growth; and, as such, they must be taken care of. But later, when this physical weakness is mostly overcome, the spirit of sacrifice and first love often disappears as well from the parents' hearts.

When it comes to helping the child in his psychic and spiritual needs we often see an almost contrary attitude in the parents. Without their being properly aware of it, the struggle with the child now begins. They consider him too much as a possession and treat him as such. Now they consider that the child should be what *they* wish him to be. Children ought to find pleasure in and be interested in what their parents choose to impose on them. They should be pleased with an environment created exclusively to suit the interests and practical comfort of adults. Parents now pay less attention to what the child needs for his spiritual development than what will "make him good and keep still."

In the psychic field those expressions in the child which manifest his true and profound needs are no longer heeded. In fact, those needs are no longer understood. Ready as educators are to respond as well as they can to the child's physical needs, they are equally reluctant when it is a question of listening to the call of his psychic needs. Prompt as they are to do what they can to help the growth of the body by procuring for it proper nourishment, cleanliness, light and fresh air, they show themselves correspondingly inert when it comes to the recognition of those laws which govern a healthy psychic development—laws which one cannot overlook without causing serious damage to mental health.

When parents observe the negative reactions which follow on a particular physical treatment they have meted out to the child, they accept them at once as a warning that they have acted contrary to the child's real necessities, and they immediately seek to find out what is the child's real need. But, on the other hand, negative reactions to certain pedagogic treatments hardly attract attention as a serious warning of the presence of some pedagogical error.

When it is observed that the child reacts by withdrawing into himself, turning away from his parents, displaying inertia, discouragement, capriciousness and other unexpected behavior, the adults in charge seldom draw the conclusion that they are in the presence of a cry or a protest from nature—whether it is a cry to the educators to discover if they have not imposed on the child something very repugnant to him, or whether they have deprived him of something which is indispensable to his development. No! Rather they consider such manifestations as a proof of a bad will (naughtiness) and as the expression of a nature under the influence of original sin, which has to be suppressed.

When we, however, defend the position that the true needs of the child's psychic development should be known and satisfied there are those who say that we are promoting a soft method which pampers the child; whereas, the very same persons would raise no objection to satisfying the requirements of physical hygiene.

Yet the urgent requirements of psychic hygiene deserve at least as much care as those of physical hygiene. If educators, instead of hindering the child's psychic development, allowed themselves to be guided by his true needs, the child's life would be more profoundly influenced, and for a longer time, by the special mentality and the special environment required by these needs.

Then civilization would not develop exclusively from the point of view of what is convenient and useful for adult life. Today, progress is sought for, too much and too exclusively, through adult qualities. Thus, civilization is based on the triumph of force, on violent conquest, on adaptation, on the struggle for existence and the survival of the conquerors. The sad consequences of this development show themselves in the religious-moral field, in social economics and in international politics. All these things are a living proof that in the construction of society something—some essential element—has been missing; that the characteristics of the child have had too little influence, because he and the adult have been too far apart. The child has almost disappeared from the thoughts of the adult world, and the adults live too much as though there were no children who have the right to influence them.

In spite of all these pedagogical errors, resulting in great measure from a lack of understanding of the child's soul, in families that are truly Christian, the idea has still remained dominant that parents exist for their children and should live mainly with them and in their service. But in the world at large—the world, that is, which has largely alienated itself from Christianity—the child and his needs and his true value are little considered. Problems such as matrimonial infidelity and divorce are discussed, described, and shown on the screen while the problem of the child and his rights and their solution remain almost completely ignored.

In certain sections of society the child has come to be regarded merely as a possession, to be acquired or not according to one's own inclinations. One or two children—yes, that is pleasant—so that one does not feel too lonely, and can amuse oneself with these doll-playthings! In this degenerate world the child is there for the adult; and, therefore, the child must live the kind of life which fits in with the picture of life which is pleasant to the adults. Their own pastimes and pleasures, their own freedom and individual requirements—these are the things which determine the way of life of the adults, whereas it should rather be determined by the needs of their children.

This abnormal condition has naturally destroyed almost all of the formative influence of the child on life, because adults have turned away from it; and, furthermore, because children themselves—treated as if they had no rights and therefore neglected—have also lost their natural grace and charm. Because children thus play an inferior part in the life of adults, the life of the latter has degenerated. The true nature of fatherhood and motherhood has been lost and so the child also has degenerated. If the child and his "rights" do not re-enter into life even the dignity of the adult will be lost forever.

It is true that, in this destructive age, something is being done toward reconstruction, toward the renewal of man and the rebuilding of his social life. But we must not persist in still seeking for that something always among adults and their works. It is necessary to have recourse to that other essential element which must intervene in the world. That element which is the origin of every man—the child.

If we were to change the center of civilization from the adult to the child a more noble form of civilization would arise. Then the education of the new generation would be the fulcrum, the central point: and to be and become a man, to be and become a Christian would be the supreme value to which all other external values would be subordinated—because looked upon as the necessary means to the attainment of the greatest possible perfection in man himself.

Respect for God in the Child

The mother and father speak of "our child," and they justify this manner of speaking by the affirmation that it is they who have brought the child to the light of day. But deep down, in their illuminated conscience, parents are aware of a deeper reason for their feeling of responsibility toward the child who has been committed to their care.

While on the one hand the first statement is true—that parents have procreated their children—no one would consider the child simply as a product of man, nor as simply just a piece of property which had created itself. Parents, especially the mother, are vividly conscious that they have played an insignificant part in the process of conception and birth, compared with that accomplished by nature. In fact the germ cells from which the child develops are not called into being by an arbitrary act of man. The union of the germ cells is more an operation of nature than that of the parents; though the latter must have fulfilled a voluntary act as a necessary introduction to it. It is not the mother who brings about the growth of the child in her womb; this is accomplished by the power of the same Being who created it in her. Nor is it the mother who accomplishes the birth of the baby; this marvelous act is performed by nature and only seconded by the mother.

It is just because God has fixed the manner of conception, development and birth in this way that the parents feel such a deep natural respect in the presence of this child who has come to them in this mysterious fashion. This respect is increased when they realize another truth—that the principal part of man, his soul, does not come from man at all, but is created directly by God.

The thought that God made a being grow within and from us in such a mysterious manner, while our own contribution is so small, easily provokes in us a great respect. Any work accomplished by God and nature always demands a deeper respect than what we do solely by ourselves.

But we shall be conscious of an even deeper respect for the child when we fully realize what he represents to us after his baptism. When the child has been baptized—and therefore, his nature, contaminated by original sin, has been buried in the sepulcher of the baptismal font—and when he rises to a new life in Christ by virtue of Christ's fruitful death, then we welcome him anew. He is now reborn directly from God, participating in God's own nature, and as God's true son— called to the possession of the divine life in an ever more perfect form.

The parents who consider the child in this way will tremble with respect before him because they now see God in him. They will no longer consider the child as something begotten by themselves alone and, as such, their property to do with as they please. They will rather be vividly conscious, instead, that the child belongs to God rather than to them, existing for God rather than for them, and that they have received from God's own hand this dependent and helpless infant in order that they, as God's helpers, may rear this new child of God according to the divine plan.

God makes known His plans to us in various ways, now

speaking through a supernatural revelation, and now by means of the nature of the beings He has created. But, in whatever way God may reveal His will and His wishes to us, it is our duty to listen to Him always. If we find ourselves confronted with the task of assisting the growth of the child, in the natural and the supernatural spheres, then our first necessity is diligently and respectfully to search until we find the way that God Himself is pointing to us.

Now God has given to the child a nature of his own, and has fixed certain laws for his development, as much and as surely in the psychic realm as in that of the physical. Anyone who is responsible for the child's normal development should become acquainted with those laws. To turn away from them would mean to lose that direction which God, as the guide of the child, gives us.

To discover the laws of the child's development would be the same thing as to discover the Spirit and Wisdom of God operating in the child. We must respect the child's objective needs as something which God Himself has commanded us to satisfy. This is the true mentality for the educator—that is, the recognition of the Divine Wisdom as a necessary element in his work as an educator.

When we recognize in the appeal of nature, the appeal of God Himself summoning us to assist the child, then we shall always be ready to comply with the child's needs. Then we shall see how, in this way, we are placing ourselves at the service of God's plans and collaborating with the work of God in the child. Then we shall not feel it a burden to adapt and sacrifice ourselves to the desires and needs of this child who has been entrusted to us. It will seem to us rather that we are responding to the will of God as manifested to us in the child. Only the full recognition of God and His rights, His requirements and His wishes with regard to children, will render us capable of living truly for the child and renouncing ourselves.

The secular approach sometimes pompously talks about respect for the child. But, in view of our egotism and our desire for domination and power, true respect for the child is only possible when we have respect for God in the child. The individual who does not believe in God—the beginning and end of all things—and who, therefore, comes to consider man himself as the supreme being, inexorably falls into a tyrannical attitude toward the child. Without question, he will begin, under the appearance of genuine concern, a real struggle with the child in order to force him into what *he himself* considers as the ideal.

What we observe in public life can also be seen in education. Where the will of God is not followed as the directive, the strong man treats the weak as a being without rights, because it is he—the Director—who determines the destiny of his subjects. If in a society without faith there is no actual arbitrary abuse of power by those who hold the reins, one will then find that the respect for the child has been violated in some other way. Then you may find they show a respect without discrimination for everything they find in the child, thus degrading him into a being who is incapable of blowing and of following an objective ideal. Indeed, it would not be easy to show less respect for the child than by treating him as a being who has no personal requirements. True respect for the child recognizes an ideal which God wishes to make actual in him.

Not only in the natural but also in the supernatural order there exists an ideal to be realized. Just as the education of physical and psychic life is nothing else than co-operation with the natural forces of growth, so the supernatural education is nothing else than co-operation with God's grace, which provides the real urge to true process of growth in the divine life.

Now supernatural growth is linked up with the use of those means which God Himself has determined, of which the sacraments and prayer are the most important. It is completely contrary to the laws of supernatural development to consider those means used for natural education as equivalent to those required for supernatural education.

Although it is true that from the thorns (of nature) you cannot gather the grapes (of the supernatural) we should not conclude from this that supernatural development would be equally guaranteed under every kind of good natural conditions.

The educator should, therefore, ascertain most minutely what are the circumstances and conditions—inside and outside the child—most favorable to the opening up of the child's soul to supernatural influences, to the vigorous and lasting co-operation with the grace of God.

A deeper respect for the nature of the child in his education in the supernatural life will produce greater success. The educator who does not believe that children feel the truths of faith in a somewhat different manner from adults, and who does not realize that children need other ways than ours to express their hope and their love for God—such a one will not be able to guide the child in a manner suitable to his religious needs.

The child must be permitted to penetrate into his supernatural life in his own peculiar manner. Even in the presence of God the child must remain a child. God Himself wants it that way and that is precisely why He created him as a child. Respect for the child's nature, which God Himself demands of us, compels us to search most carefully for those conditions in which children can abandon themselves most easily to God. Furthermore—through the influence of the same enlightening and compelling grace—the child will reveal to us, in certain moments, how he makes his own approach to God.

This discovery will be a great joy to us and, after those needs have been revealed to us, we must make every possible effort to create those conditions which are adapted to their satisfaction.

We shall then probably have to create an altogether different environment[1] and we shall also have to modify considerably our own personal attitude toward the child. But the results will easily outweigh any sacrifices because, in thus giving the child the full opportunity to live his own religious life, we shall realize that religion will have much deeper roots in his soul, and will depend much less on the stimulus of the teacher. Furthermore, the religious life of the children will also animate the religious life of the adults, because it will be more true and more real.

When we have learned to respect the child's own religious life, and have realized its lofty seriousness, we would never dream of smiling if a small child with a tender spontaneity offers a consoling gift to Jesus, crucified. Nor should we betray in any manner—by word, look or gesture—that such actions strike us as something out of the way. Neither by admiration, praise or encouragement should we disturb this beautiful spontaneity, because we shall have learned to look upon such manifestations as the natural form of expression at this particular phase of his life.

Along with the acquisition of a truer and deeper respect for the rights and needs of the child, we shall find that our own attitude toward him will also change considerably. Harshness, stern commands and arbitrary prohibitions,

---

[1] The Atrium—Ed.

which are often given more because we are in a bad humor than with any educational purpose, will disappear. We shall know better how to carry out St. Paul's practical advice to the Ephesians: "Fathers, provoke not your children to anger." The Encyclical of Pope Pius XI "On the Christian Education of Youth" explains that this provocation to anger arises most from the fact that parents have too little patience to put up with the spontaneity and innate vivacity of their children. We need to understand why the Holy Father exhorts us to an ever greater respect for the child's nature.

We shall learn to resist that vanity which urges us to boast, only too willingly, about our children's accomplishments—even about their acts of prayer—because their natural simplicity will be something too sacred for us to violate. We shall be on our guard against that impatience which forces children into doing things of which they are not really capable, lest their failure result in a complex of fear and timidity. We would urge such parents to emulate the patience of Mary, the Mother of the Divine Child, who knew how to wait, with all humility, for His miracles.

If respect for the child were more general we would be on our guard against doing (in our impatience) things for the child which he could very well do for himself at his own slower rhythm, and take the greatest delight in so doing. Respect for the child's laws of growth would prevent us from the temptation to push children on at the utmost speed in order to have them act, prematurely, as adults. In any case this would be useless because to become truly an adult, it is necessary for the child first to have lived through the natural phases of childhood. One becomes a well-balanced adult only if one has fully been a child.

On the other hand, our respect for the child's right to progress gradually along the path of growth would prevent us from trying to hold him back, and keep him in a phase of development that he would naturally wish to outgrow. To fondle a child, as if he were still a baby of a few months, does not correspond to the natural needs of a seven-year-old. The tendency on the part of the adult to behave in this way comes from the understandable—but no longer admissible—need of the educator to keep the child in a state of infantile dependence, in order that the adult may enjoy the feeling of being continuously indispensable.

Lack of respect for the child's rights of development often brings the educator to treat the child in the manner which is most pleasing to him. The somewhat pathetic complaint, "I notice that my son seems to be getting tired of me and has less need of me; I feel that I am actually losing him," proves how painful it is not to be able to keep one's child as if he were one's own possession.

Respect for these needs of development are all the more absolutely necessary because children, in their first infancy, are particularly vulnerable both physically and psychically. Deviations and sicknesses then most easily occur, which might render psychic and physical development exceedingly difficult. It is only in recent times that we have clearly understood this truth.

Christ and the Child

The respect which we demand for the child we demand in the name of the Divine Friend of children.

First of all, we should like to point out the severity shown by Jesus toward any adults who became a cause of scandal to children—a severity almost as great as that which He displayed in the Temple courts to those adults who profaned the house of God itself. To those who offend the innocence of children, and thus profane the spiritual temple of God, He said, "If anyone hurts the conscience of one of these little ones that believe in Me he had better have been drowned in the depths of the sea with a millstone about his neck" *(Matthew 18, 6)*.

Jesus not only addresses a severe warning to those who irritate or anger children but He will not suffer to see them despised. "See to it that you do not treat one of these little ones with contempt."

How much contempt is often manifested when people say, "Oh, that's only a kids' affair"; and with these words they seek to excuse all kinds of impoliteness, injustice, and negligence toward the children under their charge.

In the spirit of Jesus one would look in vain for any reason for considering children as "only children." Very impressive is the reason He gives why we should not despise them—"Because I tell you they have angels of their own who continually behold the face of My Father in heaven." And thus Jesus teaches us that we should indeed respect these little ones because God Himself does so in a high degree, giving to each one of them his own angel in heaven as their protector.

This respect, which He demands in us, Christ Himself shows in His own example. While He is expounding to the learned and noble Jews His elevated doctrine with regard to marriage some children arrive on the scene and would like to approach Him. The disciples, wishing to keep them at a distance, send them away. "These children have no business being here while Jesus is discoursing with the noble Hebrews"—so must the disciples have reasoned it out. But the Divine Friend of the little children thinks otherwise. He shows Himself indignant, and, with annoyance in His voice, says, "Let the little children come to Me and do not hinder them." And His reason? "For of such is the kingdom of heaven." Then Jesus put his arms around them and, as a sign of His blessing, He lays His hand upon them. In the Gospel according to Mark we read still further the following words of Jesus, "I tell you truly that the man who does not accept the kingdom of God as a little child will not enter into it" (Mark 10, 15). The simplicity with which the child receives the divine secrets is given to us as an example of what our own attitude should be; and in this sense, then, the child is put before us as the guide who unconsciously shows us the way.

On another occasion the apostles manifest once again their aspirations toward a privileged post in the kingdom of heaven. When they asked Jesus to tell them who will be the greatest, He called to His side a little child, to whom He gave a place in the midst of them, saying, "Unless you be converted and become as little children you shall not enter the kingdom of heaven" (Matthew 18, 3). And elsewhere added, "He who is the least among you shall be the greatest" (Luke 9, 48).

A person's respect for another shows itself best when, not regarding himself as superior to the other, he makes himself an equal. And this is precisely what the Son of God did when He preferred to come into the world as a child, and live through all the phases of infantile life. So now he who despises the little ones because they are "only children" should be aware of his lack of respect, because in despising the child as a child, he is also denigrating Christ.

That the child exercises a special influence because he is a child, we see also in the case of the Child Jesus. No one will deny that the feast of the birth of Christ—the same Christ who, as an adult, died and rose again—influences us in a different manner from that of Easter. At Christmas it is the child that governs us; at Christmas we are overcome by the weakness, helplessness and tenderness of the child. Then we ourselves become small and good. The Child Omnipotent, who has made Himself defenseless, disarms us. Who is not filled with wonder that the shepherds, on returning to their sheep, saw the joy of Peace on Earth of which the angels sang, come down to earth in a child!

Probably the Child Jesus speaks to some in accents even more touching and impressive than He does as an adult. Thinking of the Christ Child we can learn how to abandon our own tyrannical behavior toward children. In the strength of our respectful love—which we now at times consider to be weakness—we shall see the true significance of being an adult. The means by which the child influences us, *his* respectful love, so full of confidence, will then become our great strength in the educational field. Imitating our Divine Master we shall not let ourselves be motivated by the impulse to pomp and power, but by the respect for Christ-in-the-child, who—with our help—must grow into the fullness of his personality.

On one occasion Christ spoke certain words by which he practically identified Himself with children: "He who welcomes this little child in My name welcomes Me; and he who welcomes Me welcomes Him that sent Me" (Luke 9, 48). Let us then see Christ and the Father in the child, and our attitude toward him will be profound and sacred. And as forerunners of Christ-in-the-child, we shall be able to say with sincerity, as did John the Baptist—"He must increase and I must decrease."

CHAPTER TWO

THE LIFE OF THE CHILD
WITHIN THE CHURCH

*". . . . from the altar I implore the dear and all-powerful
children to stretch out their helping hands to me."—*
BENEDICT XV.

When, at Barcelona, we began religious education in the
"Model Montessori School," not only had our plan
of action been long and well considered, but a significant
incident was connected with what eventually transpired.

Father Casulleras, a Vincentian priest, came back from
Guatemala in 1909. He was filled with the conviction that the
child should be brought into the church, to live and grow up
there, since the church is the true place of education for him.
In the different towns of the Balearic Isles, where, as superior,
he directed the Fathers of the Mission and the Sisters of
Charity, he spoke of the necessity of having "Houses for the
Children" within the protecting shadow of the church. He
had not yet heard of my "Children's Houses" in Rome, and it
was only in 1910 that, by chance, he came across my book in
which I describe them. To Padre Casulleras the coincidence
of names seemed providential, and, having read the account

of my method, he judged it suited to his "Children's Houses." Straightway, he went to speak of the matter to Father Clascar, the chaplain of the Children's Home at Barcelona. Father Clascar was a learned man, who had translated the Bible and the Psalms into the Catalan vernacular, and who was one of the founders of the Institute of Catalan Studies. They immediately agreed to apply my method to the children of the Home. They did so not only there but in all the orphanages of the Balearic Isles conducted by the Sisters of Charity of St. Vincent de Paul.

Although these priests neither knew me, nor knew that I was a Catholic, and although in my book I made no direct profession of religious faith, it seemed to them that in its very substance my method was apostolic. It was not until later when we came into personal touch that we spoke of the importance of attempting to apply the principles of my method directly to religious education.

The Abbot of the celebrated Benedictine Sanctuary of Our Lady of Montserrat welcomed this idea and invited my colleague, Anna Maccheroni, to take part in a Liturgical Congress which was held in the Basilica of Montserrat. The pedagogical problem set before us had, in reality, already been indicated and fundamentally solved by the Holy Father, Pius X. In his Decree on the Communion of Children, he expressed the wish that they should be admitted to an earlier participation in the holy mysteries than was usual at that time.

Another fundamental point, too, which bears on "technical pedagogy" was indicated by the holy Pontiff, in the words "Let us educate the people to take a more active participation in the liturgy"; along with the rest of our faithful, little children were to be admitted to the most intimate and sublime act of religious life—communion with Jesus Christ.

The liturgy, magnificent expression of the content of the faith, may well be called "the pedagogical method" of the Church which, not satisfied with teaching by means of the word preached to the faithful, makes the various acts of religion real, makes them come to life, and allows the people to take part in them each day. And to find life-giving spiritual nourishment the child has only to open the windows of his soul to the light of the liturgy and all it embodies of divine grace.

But if the adult needs not only to know but to "live" his religion, the need is all the greater for the child—who is more adapted to live it than to know it. Are not the limits of the problem concerning the religious education of the child identical with those of the various methods of learning and memorizing? In fact, knowledge in our case is nothing else but the first indispensable step in opening the paths of life to the soul.

Here, then, is a necessary complement of the religious instruction of the child: *make the liturgy accessible to children*. The impressive ceremonies of the Church, the sacred symbolism, the deep significance underlying everything, the exact use and end of all the objects, the systematic distribution of the various liturgical roles—all give a fundamental importance to the place where the faithful meet—and, at the same time, afford sensible means, such as lights, colors, sounds, which help the soul, just as benches and kneelers assist the body, to remain long in church without becoming fatigued.

Now this was precisely the argument offered by Anna Maccheroni in the Church of Montserrat. She affirmed before the whole Congress, which comprised all the clergy of Catalonia, that the teaching of the liturgy as the illustration of Christian doctrine—as set forth by Bishop Ridolfi of

Vincenza, approved by St. Pius X, and distributed in various books for children of different ages—could be presented to children at a much earlier age than the one called for. She added that she was ready to try the experiment in the Montessori School of Barcelona which received children from three to six years of age. Signorina Maccheroni's discourse was approved, it remains as an historic document in our educational method.[2]

The result was the opening of "The Children's House in the Church," founded by Father Casulleras, and a new life began there—that of "The Little Ones Living in the Church." At the same time, the Montessori Method was furnished with a long-sought opportunity of penetrating deeper into the life of the child's soul, and of thus fulfilling its true educational mission.

The first step was "to prepare the place" for the *bambini* ... the chapel, which had to be the most beautiful room in the house. The Provincial Deputation of Barcelona, fired with the enthusiasm of Enrico Prat de la Riba (who died before he completed his noble project), engaged distinguished artists to adorn the "Children's Chapel" in white and gold, the walls being furnished with hangings of yellow damask. Suitable seats, holy water fonts within easy reach, pictures, and small statues placed a yard from the ground indicated that the new Lilliputians were invited to become "active members" of the Church.

A young priest, Mossèn Iginio Angèles, was chosen as chaplain because of his simple, pure and ardent faith as the apostle of our younger children.

Father Angèles, deeply moved, began to officiate and to preach in this unusual church, and what followed became a

---

[2] The Liturgy and the Pedagogical Teaching of the Liturgy," in *Report of the Liturgical Congress of Montserrat.*

witness to grace. One could see how little children, because of their innocence, can feel the need of God's presence in a purer and more intense manner, even if less definitely than adults. Their souls seem to be more open to divine intuitions than those of adults, despite their less perfectly developed intelligence and skill in reasoning.

Meanwhile, the application of the method followed in my "Children's Houses" produced this excellent fruit—the Church almost seemed to be the end of the education which the method proposed to give. The "silence" observed in class, to accustom the child to recollection, here found its application. It became the interior recollection observed in the House of God, amid the gentle nickering of the candlelight in an atmosphere dim, yet resplendent with gleaming white and gold. Again, their actions were practically repetitions of what they had learned to do in the classroom; walking silently, placing chairs quietly, standing up and sitting down gracefully and passing between benches and bystanders without knocking against them. They carried fragile objects with care, such as candles without spilling wax on their clothes, baskets of flowers or vases of water to be filled with flowers and placed at the foot of the altar.

Such things, therefore, must appeal to their tender minds as the end of effort patiently sustained, giving them a pleasing sense of joy and of new dignity. Before such an apprenticeship, these tiny members of the Church feel that they are servants executing material tasks without understanding what they do; after it, and after what they have learned has been applied in church, they begin to comprehend and to distinguish between the different circumstances.

In order to grasp this idea one ought to know the Montessori Method in the "Children's Houses," which prepares the children in the daily life of the classroom by exercises which are, in themselves, quite independent of religious education, but which seem to be a preparation for it. In fact, they aid in perfecting the child, in making him calm, obedient, attentive to his own movements, capable of silence and recollection.

When this preparation has been made, the child finds in the church an application which is attractive, varied and deeply significant; and as a result he receives a sense of dignity and satisfaction. The child of four is not ignorant of the difference between the holy water font into which he puts his fingers before blessing himself, and the basin in the next room where he washes his hands. Now this appreciation of the difference between like things is a real, intellectual labor which the little creature initiates when he begins to realize that he is a child of God, lovingly received in the house of his great heavenly Father, though hitherto he has been considered almost incapable of rising to any such idea or concept.

Later I would come across some opposition to the reality of such impressions. "Do you know why my little nephew wants to go to school in time for Mass? Because you let him put out the candles. That is all! Would it not be better to apply this pleasing exercise to arithmetic? For example, have him hold ten lighted candles and then put them out counting one, two, three, etc."

The critic who spoke thus had, of course, a poor spiritual understanding and little knowledge of children. The arithmetical exercise with the candles would have lasted at most a week, the time necessary, more or less, to learn to count from one to ten. But those children, as they grew older and continued their instruction either in general or religious knowledge, would observe in church the putting out of the candles that consume themselves, burning in the presence of Jesus descended among them. And they would understand that the act was not a mere childish pastime but a religious function to be reverently fulfilled, because done in a sacred place and bearing upon the worship paid to God.

When Father Angèles began to explain the sacraments, he wished to address himself to the older children only, but the younger ones would not go away, and followed his words with the greatest attention. This truly extraordinary priest seemed born for the mission, and even the children of three followed him spellbound. He prepared the baptismal font, and whatever was necessary for the ritual; chose the godfather and godmother from among the children themselves; asked someone to bring a doll, over whom he performed, step by step, the rites used in the administration of this great sacrament. On other occasions, an older child acted as a catechumen and asked for baptism. The children showed keen interest in learning that baptism in the early days of the Church was conferred on adults, and that, to them, it is still given when they are converted to Catholicism. Thus, they gathered, little by little, their first notions of the liturgy. They understood, for example, how the Mass is the representation, par excellence, of the Passion and death of Christ; the older among them served Mass; and the younger came at the Offertory, or Preparation of the Gifts, bringing their gifts to the altar, and when the Divine Sacrifice was over they extinguished the candles.[3] By such means, when the time for first Communion comes, the children find that they have already "lived in the Church" for three or four years. Considering their tender age, they have a knowledge of religious things which is quite unusual.

[3] Under the liturgical reforms begun by the Second Vatican Council, a parish Sunday Mass which is offered in keeping with the spirit of renewal will provide vastly greater opportunities for young children to grasp the meaning of what they see. They will soon learn the words of the hymns; they can, in many parishes, place their own host in the ciborium before Mass; they see altars much more closely approximating real tables; they hear much in their own language.—Ed.

Religiously inclined, and already trained to independence, these children prove themselves to be exceptionally "strong and robust" souls, just as the bodies of well-nourished, well-cared-for children are robust. Growing up in this way, they display neither shyness nor fear, nor credulity. They show a pleasing ease and grace of manner, courage, accurate knowledge of things, faith above all in life and in God.

The Preparation of the Gifts

In order to make the children understand and remember that the Mass represents an offering, a sacrifice (to make sacred a thing which is separated from others in order to pay homage to the majesty of God), and consequently differs from such devotions as the Way of the Cross, Benediction, etc., the children themselves prepare and offer the species: they cultivate the grain and the vine; they make the hosts, and then they offer the bread and wine at the altar when Mass is being celebrated.

Part of a large meadow, in which the children used to play after lunch, was set aside for the cultivation of the wheat and the grapes.

Two rectangles were chosen by the children themselves, one to the right, the other to the left of the meadow. A grain that ripens quickly was selected. Into the prepared furrows, each child cast a few seeds, so that all sowed some. The movements for sowing, care that the seeds should not fall outside the furrow, the gravity and solemnity with which the outdoor ceremony was conducted—everything made them immediately understand how the act was suited to the end proposed.

Shortly after, the vines were planted. They looked like dry roots and gave little promise of the wonder the children were led to expect— namely the appearance one day of real clusters of grapes. The young shoots were placed in a trench in parallel lines, the plants being equi-distant. The two little fields had to be enclosed. It seemed best to plant flowers all round as a perpetual homage of fragrance and beauty to the vines that would ripen and give fruit, one day to become the matter for the Eucharistic Consecration. The children continued to play in the other part of the meadow; they ran, played ball, and in their merriment they gave glory to God.

With the joy of playing was mingled the deeper sentiment of assisting daily at the marvel of growth. In the wheat field parallel lines of green soon began to appear, and the grain grew and rose up, awakening the keenest interest in the children. At last even the dry grape shoots began to put forth tiny, pale leaves. The children gathered round, observing. Some were chosen to disinfect the vine-plants. When the wonderful clusters appeared, they covered them with white netting to guard them against insects and birds.

It was decided that for the opening and closing of the school year, two out-of-door feasts should be established: one corresponding to the harvest, the other to the vintage. These feasts, we thought, might be brightened by rustic music on primitive instruments and by folk songs, some of which were so harmonious that in ancient times the tunes were taken over for the sacred hymns of the Church. A doubt then arose: could the reaping be done by the children themselves? The yellow fruit richly laden was all in a line, and the children were quivering with anticipation, so we decided to trust to their prudence.

Just as at table, relying on their movement and will-training, we had placed a knife in their hands, so now we entrusted the scythe to them—tiny scythes, made on purpose, with gleaming white handles.

Everything went well. With care, with evident pleasure, with emotion perhaps deeper still, they cut all the wheat. Next came the solemn joy of making the sheaves, binding them with colored ribbons, placing them in rows, then bidding them farewell, to await their return as flour.

Meanwhile they learned to operate the machines for making the hosts and for cutting the large and small circles.

The idea seemed so good that the Bishop decided to incorporate it in the solemn procession of Corpus Christi; in Barcelona and its suburbs, hosts cut by the children's hands, and made of the flour from that seed which the children had grown, were offered at Mass.

The children united in choosing the bearers of the offering, who were appropriately dressed, the little girls wearing white veils. Two-handled jars were used for carrying the water and the wine. The children marched in line carrying the offerings in small baskets, or on rush plates covered with little cloths ornamented with lace. Later, those who wished to communicate at Mass offered their hosts at the altar rails where they were afterwards to receive Holy Communion.

Preparation for Communion

The children who are judged ready for first Communion are selected. The final group of chosen ones is determined after consultation between the family and the school. The children, who assist at and take part in the religious exercises, beg to be admitted to first Communion at six, or even five.

The choice of the candidates for first Communion is a great event for the whole school; the children are the object of the love and protection of everybody; their names are printed on cards with a petition for prayers that they may be really ready to receive our Lord. Each classroom, the chapel, even the entrance to the school has one of these cards affixed to the wall, so that all who enter are informed of what is about to take place, in order that they may unite in prayer. Every day their companions are reminded of the need of divine help for those chosen for the reception of the Eucharist. The preparation lasts five weeks. Each of these weeks begin at 10 a.m. on Saturday—a day on which there is little school work.

Every Saturday, therefore, a collective ceremony is held at which all the children, big and small, the teaching and the serving staffs assist. All gather around the future communicants to help them, to support them by their presence and their prayers, and to rejoice with them. A priest stands between the altar and the communion-rail, the communicants to right and left. On the table of offering are lighted candles and various objects connected with the lesson of the day: such as a facsimile of the Tablet of Moses or a fisherman's net. After a few words of explanation, the priest solemnly bestows upon each of the communicants a sheet artistically printed and adorned by a picture.

On this text, presented with such solemnity, will hinge the religious instruction of the whole week; and, at the end, the five sheets bound together will make a souvenir book of their first Communion.

During the week the children memorize essential catechetical doctrine: the Creed, the Commandments, etc.

The following Saturday, one by one, clearly and distinctly, they recite what they have learned, before the altar and in the presence of all.

Their companions and teachers pray for them and sing a hymn. The pages given to them on the five consecutive Saturdays contain the following points:

1. Faith, dogma—*The Creed.*
2. Love, charity—*The Commandments.*

3. Prayer—*Our Father, Hail Mary, Glory Be.*
4. The Sacraments—*Baptism, Confession, Communion.*
5. The Good News—*Epistles and Gospels.*

In the last week the children go into retreat for five days before their first Communion—Monday through Friday. They live apart from their companions, and a portion of the garden is set aside and reserved for them. In the classrooms, too, they are separated. They dine in school alone and recollected. This isolation is, however, neither sad nor wearisome, for innumerable proofs of love reach the small solitaries.

Meanwhile, the older boys in the school give all their attention to the preparation for the solemn Mass, sung in Gregorian chant; and the music being practiced in their honor sweetly reaches the ears of the future communicants. During retreat, the children laugh and work. Special and tender care surrounds them. They pass the greater part of the time in the garden, looking after the plants and the animals.

Other manual work consists in making their own silver rosaries which they will use on their first Communion day, and they themselves bind in book form the five sheets they have prepared.

Physical exercises suited to the occasion consist in practicing standing up and sitting down, walking quietly without knocking against people or objects, genuflecting, kneeling down and rising up; in observing silence, in maintaining dignity, in not turning at a noise. The occupation of the heart consists in raising their thoughts to God at every action during the day, in loving and praising Him.

The suitability of a five-day retreat for little children was well considered and discussed before the experiment was tried. I had faith in the dispositions developed by their education which had made them patient and tranquil students—already given to a kind of spontaneous meditation by the "cycle of work"[4]—observers of external things and therefore capable of finding satisfaction for themselves; lovers of silence, and the stillness which produces it; attentive to the little movements of their own muscles and capable of controlling them. Such children are ready to go a step further and apply the directions to their own interior actions. Not only do the principles of human justice interest them, but a simple love of Jesus is born in their hearts and with it a great desire of purification. The soul of the child is capable of high aspirations which are reflected in his behavior and in his acts. We have many proofs of this, in diverse conditions and places.

This retreat of our first communicants represents a temporary separation of their group from the rest of their school companions, who are engaged in various tasks, and therefore capable of involuntarily disturbing their concentration. But it is not a life of complete sacrifice and absolute interior recollection that is expected of them; they are left free for their own amusements and are to be seen for the greater part of the time in the garden, amid the blossoming flowers of May, picking little bouquets or scented grasses which they carry to Christ.

During class they are quietly entertained by slides of sacred persons, places and events. Illustrated books and collections of picture cards are at their disposal. Much time is spent in setting the table for dinner, in clearing away and washing the dishes, and in putting everything in its proper place. Making the rosary, which begins with the choice of necessary objects and the picking out of the silver beads, provides a restful and

---

[4] We give the name "cycle of work" to the series of actions performed by the child when, according to my method, he spontaneously chooses his work from the apparatus put within his reach.

interesting occupation. Then at times, prayer breaks forth as a necessity; little processions are organized in the garden; the singing of a hymn is readily undertaken.

On the morning of the great Saturday the church is decorated by the older children with candles and flowers. Only their parents—who in Spain are accustomed to take part in the ceremony—are admitted to the chapel. (With something of the solemnity of a wedding, they give the children a ring as a symbol of their union with Christ. After Communion the children continue to wear this ring.) The communicants in simple white attire, carrying their silver rosaries, wait in a room distant from the chapel. Their classmates, from whom they have been separated for almost a week, go in solemn procession to greet them and conduct them to the altar. The priest, in his sacred vestments, leads the way. He is followed by two acolytes in surplices, with cross and candles. Behind them come all the children of the school, carrying lighted candles. The procession sets forth from the altar, passing between the rows of parents and proceeds, singing, to the room where the waiting communicants hear the strains draw near, and see the long line of lights approach.

Then the procession returns. This time immediately behind the cross come the first communicants, followed by their companions, still carrying the lighted candles and singing until the former reach the altar where Christ awaits them.

This act of homage and love has touched the hearts of many priests, and the custom of going for the communicants, and accompanying them processionally to the altar with hymns of joy, has already been adopted in various religious institutions in Barcelona.

The afternoon is given over to religious festivities, beginning with the Litany of Our Lady which the children intone on the terrace, while the parents and their numerous friends and acquaintances answer from the garden. Then there is a procession in which all the children, dressed in white, take part. The older children carry lighted tapers while the smaller carry white lilies. Some bear on their shoulders a statue of the Infant Jesus resting on a bed of fresh flowers, and others hold a banner of our Lady.

The day ends with an *agape*: a meal shared in love.

CHAPTER THREE

THE ATRIUM OR CHILDREN'S CHAPEL

Doctor Montessori was well aware that her work in Barcelona constituted merely a beginning. She herself modestly spoke of it as un tentative She hoped some day to complete the work thus begun, and had already mapped out the lines along which she would have it develop.

In the meantime there are many teachers who are anxious to apply her principles without delay to the religious education of the children under their care. For these Doctor Montessori authorized the editor to publish the substance of a series of conversations which he had with her in May, 1927, on this subject. The following dialogue is based on notes taken at the time.

Question: In your method you have prepared the environment of the child in such a way as to stimulate the development of the natural faculties. What sort of environment would you prepare to correspond with, and draw out the development of the supernatural faculties?

Dr. Montessori: Such an environment already exists. It is the Church. What is the Church if it is not a specially prepared environment for drawing out and sustaining the supernatural life of man?

Question: But speaking practically, as a teacher, how would you set about giving what is called "religious instruction"?

Dr. Montessori: People are constantly asking me about this question of religious instruction—whether it should be long or short, determined by the teacher, or left to the choice of the children, and so on. They nearly always speak of it as if it were a special school "subject."

My answer to all this is that I should not regard it as a "subject" at all. The preparation of the child for his full participation in the life of the Church is a much wider thing than the learning by heart of certain intellectual truths. *It is a life in itself.*

The child, for instance, must learn how to make the Sign of the Cross, how and when to genuflect, how to carry objects such as candles and flowers gracefully. He must be taught how to prepare for the sacraments of penance and of the Holy Eucharist, and how to participate in these sacraments. He must be taught how to follow the actions of the Mass, how to take part in processions and, in general, how to participate in the liturgical ceremonies of the Church, as far as it is possible for the layman to do so. All these are things to be *done* rather than things to be *read.*

In all such matters it is important that the small child should be most carefully instructed, so that he shall feel "at home" in God's House.

Learning by Heart

Question: But how about the catechism? Would you not have it learned by heart?

Dr. Montessori: Yes, of course, I would have certain things learned by heart; but I would have the memorizing come *at the end, as a summing up after the experience.*

Question: What do you mean by "after the experience ... at the end"?

Dr. Montessori: I mean something similar to the manner in which our children become acquainted with the definitions of geometric forms. You know how the children occupy themselves with the geometric insets in our schools. They take them out of their sockets and run their fingertips around the edges, thus getting a tactile as well as a visible impression of the various forms. They also take different kinds of geometric forms out of their drawers at the same time and mix them together. Then by comparison and contrast they sort these out again, putting each back in its right socket. All this is genuine experimental work, involving trial and error; and in this way the children become more and more familiar with the various geometric shapes. So that when they come to learn the exact definitions, one can truly say that the learning by heart comes "*at the end, after they have experienced them.*"

Question: What parts of the catechism would you have the children learn by heart?

Dr. Montessori: That I could not, naturally, decide myself. They would have to be selected by someone in authority who would also be responsible for the wording. The important thing would be to have these statements *very exact.*

It would not be necessary, in my opinion, to memorize *all* the catechism—only certain necessary and accurate definitions, the ones essential for every Catholic to know. Nowadays there are so many people who talk such a deal of sentimental rubbish about religion that it is imperative that every child should have something clear and logical to fall back on. One cannot, unfortunately, enjoin silence on all these *blabbermouths*—more's the pity!—so one must learn to distinguish between their vague ideas and exact definitions.

I am quite confident that, by teaching children religious truths according to the method I have indicated, we should be able to show that our *bambini* had grasped the truths as well as, if not better than, older children taught by the usual methods.

Question: To go back for a moment to what you said about the children learning things by heart—after they had experienced them. I can see how this can be managed in a subject like geometry, but how are you to make it work in the sphere of religious knowledge?

Dr. Montessori: For this it would be necessary to have a special material, appealing to the senses, working along the same lines as our didactic material. The children would learn by means of objects and actions.

Question: Would you have this religious apparatus mixed up with the ordinary didactic apparatus of the Montessori school, or would you keep it separate?

Dr. Montessori: I would keep it separate. I would have a separate room dedicated to the supernatural. Everything in this room would have a bearing on the spiritual life, and the general effect would be that here the soul of the child and all his activities would be centered in the life and personality of our Lord. The work in this room would of course include: Bible History, Church History, the Lives of the Saints, and the Liturgy.

Question: Do you not think it might create an artificial sense of separation in the child's mind to have all the religious material kept separate from the rest—as though the supernatural life could not go on just as well in an ordinary schoolroom?

Dr. Montessori: No, I do not think it would have this effect at all. In our adult life the church or chapel is a place especially devoted to the supernatural. Its prepared environment helps on our spiritual life; but this does not *prevent* us from having supernatural inspirations at other times, and in other places which are not so significantly set apart.

It would be better to have a room devoted to the religious life, because such broad distinctions are a help to the immature intellect, and form the basis of more detailed subdivisions. It would, of course, be possible to have the natural and the supernatural apparatus all in the same room, just as it is possible to eat, sleep, work and play all in one room; although I would suggest that it is better to have separate rooms.

Question: Might not this idea of having a separate room for the teaching of religion be looked upon as rather unnecessary and newfangled?

Dr. Montessori: People might think it was a new idea, but, as a matter of fact, it is a very old idea—almost as old as the Church itself. In the early Church there was, indeed, a special room called the *Atrium,* generally adjoining the church, which was used for the training and instruction of catechumens. It was, as you might say, a sort of anteroom to the Church, both in a literal and a metaphorical sense. Here, as in so many cases, we can, with great profit, take a "leaf out of the book" of the early Church.

This room then, which one might call the Atrium, would be set apart for the preparation of little children for their full participation in the life of the Church. It would not simply be a question of teaching them their catechism, but something much broader and deeper. This room would be a place where the religious sentiment would be born, and nurtured, where the children would be quite free in the expression of their religious instincts.

Just as my first schools in Rome were called "Children's Houses" *(Case dei Bambini),* so one might call these "Children

Churches." Not of course in the sense that they should form a substitute for the real church—which would be absurd—but because everything in them would be directed toward initiating the children into the true life of the Church.

Question: Supposing that money were no object, how would you build your Atrium or Children's Church? How would it be furnished? And how would the children behave in it?

Dr. Montessori: That is quite a big question. Well, first, I would try and find some architects and artists who understood the child spirit; and I would get them to give of their best. I have no patience with the idea that because children are very young they can be put off with the second rate. I would have the room built in an ecclesiastical style, with pointed windows, possibly of stained glass. The windows, of course, would be low, down to the children's level—like everything else in the room. There would be statues, here and there, of our Lord, our Lady and the saints; and the children would bring flowers to put in front of these images, and also light candles before them. On the walls would be sacred pictures illustrating Old and New Testament stories. The whole room would be fitted up as a sensorial environment calling out to the souls of the children. As in an ordinary Montessori school, around the walls would be cupboards and shelves with various exercises and occupations for the children to work at.

Question: What sort of of occupations would there be in this Atrium?

Dr. Montessori: My principle would be that in this room *everything that the children learn and do in the ordinary Montessori school would be repeated on a higher plane, supernaturalized so to speak.*

Question: Could you give some examples of what you

mean by this "supernaturalizing" of the activities of the ordinary school?

Dr. Montessori: Well, you know what we mean in our schools by the "exercises in practical life"—how the children are taught to take great care of their environment—how they dust the apparatus and so on. Now they would do the same here. With an even more loving care, they would busy themselves dusting the statues and pictures, the little altar and its furniture, and all the other objects in the Atrium.

Then again, as we have already mentioned, the children would feel that the skill they had acquired in carrying a glass of water without spilling it would have gained a new value and significance when they carried vases of flowers to place in front of the holy images, or carry a font full of holy water.

I would arrange, too, that the children should often have little religious processions, carrying flowers to place at our Lady's feet, or at the foot of the altar; and here again the marching while carrying things, which is a regular part of the ordinary Montessori school routine, would acquire a new meaning.

In a similar way the Silence Game—in itself so full of mystery and awe—would now become the prelude to the still more wonderful silence of prayer and meditation.

Even the decimal system, with which the little ones have just become acquainted, can be made use of here, in the counting and arranging of beads to make rosaries. There is a stage (as the children are just acquiring the notion of number) when they are interested in anything that has number and can be counted. At this stage they will begin quite spontaneously to count all sorts of things, such as the number of persons in the room, or the number of books on a shelf. It would be a simple matter to devise different exercises, of varying degrees of difficulty, in which they would be able to make use of their newly-won knowledge of numbers. They could begin with simple numbers like five loaves and two fishes, the twelve apostles, the seven churches, the number of years in our Lord's life and in His ministry, the number of candles used at low and high Mass and at Benediction. Coming to more difficult numbers, they could express numerically, with the aid of the number apparatus, such facts as the number of Sundays in the year, the different subdivisions of the liturgical year, for example, the number of Sundays in Lent or after Pentecost, etc.

They could use the thousand-bead chain as a chain of years and, by counting off the thirty-three years of our Lord's life at one end, they would be able—by marking in the centuries with number cards—to gain a clear idea as to the length of the Church's history. These are only suggestions, but one could find many facts in connection with the Church and its history which have a numerical significance, which would be specially interesting to the children at this stage.

In the Montessori School the children are busied at a certain stage with the color tablets. These exercises give them an intense interest in colors; and everything that they see in their environment which has color attracts their attention. It would be a great joy to the children, at this particular "sensitive period," to be given the little models of the liturgical vestments, in order to recognize their different colors and learn the significance of each.

Music, of course, would play an important part in the life of the Atrium. I would have the children taught how to sing the Gregorian chants, and also the old hymns which have been handed down as folk songs.

You know that our children have a special musical apparatus, made of bells, for learning the notes of the scale and their names. In the Atrium, too, I would have a set of bells, but here I would have them arranged as a little belfry, like a miniature church tower. The children who had already learned to play little tunes on the other bells would be allowed to use these at certain times. They would be used for calling the others to prayer—as at the Angelus, and on other occasions. These bells would be useful, too, in other ways. I would ask a priest to come and explain to the little ones the ceremony of Blessing the Bells. He need not necessarily actually bless the bells, but it would be easier for the children to understand the ceremony with these objects before them. They could also copy some of the passages from the prayers used at the Blessing of the Bells, which are very beautiful . . . remember? "May the sound of the bells drive away dangers, prevent storms and tempests from harming us; may their voice increase the devotion of the faithful and rouse them to eagerness in hastening to church, there to share in divine worship."

Question: Would you apply similar techniques to reading and writing?

Dr. Montessori: Many of the children in the Atrium will be at an age when they are just learning to read. For these I would devise the same kind of exercises as I have done in the ordinary school. As at Barcelona, I would have little cards made out with names written on them. These would correspond to various small objects which would be kept in sets in boxes, each set being accompanied by a small packet of cards with the names describing them. The child would take the objects out of a box, spread them out on the table, and then read the little cards, placing each under the object it denotes. One set—for the small children—might contain such objects as a cross, a lamb, a rosary, or figures representing our Lord, His Mother, St. Peter and so on.

Another set would comprise the various objects used on the altar—a chalice, a monstrance, a corporal, an altar cloth, a candlestick, a crucifix, a burse, and so forth. The different vestments worn by the priest at Holy Mass would form another series . . . still another could be made of the various things found in a church, such as a baptismal font, confessional, lectern, altar, pulpit, etc. Pictures mounted on cards could be used where it was not possible to obtain suitable models.

It would be a good thing also to make use of reading slips such as the children have in our schools. These reading slips, as I expect you remember, are in the form of little commands which the child on reading has to execute himself. The little one struggles eagerly and voluntarily with the difficulties of reading because he knows that—when he has wrested the meaning from the sentence—he will be amply rewarded. The reward lies in the joy of carrying out the action suggested by the card. To these little children, just beginning to read, it seems a great mystery that these small cards can, as it were, come to life and give commands like a living person.

Question: What kind of actions would these readings slips command the children to do?

Dr. Montessori: In such an environment as there would be in the Atrium, it would not be hard to find many things for them to do. They would carry out a variety of liturgical activities.

For instance:

1. Go to the holy water font and very devoutly make the sign of the cross.
2. Go to a statue of an angel, think of it as your guardian angel, and thank him for looking after you. Ask him to pray for you.
3. Go to a prie-dieu and say an Our Father for the pope's intention.

4. Make a little drawing of a boat with St. Peter in it. What does the boat stand for and why do you put St. Peter in it?

These are only suggestions of the sort of thing one could do; probably each directress would make up her own.

As the children get older I would encourage them to write little compositions on biblical subjects. Not indeed that they will need much encouragement; for it has often been proved that little children *prefer* writing on these subjects as their hearts are so full of love and faith.

Everything to be supernaturalized! That would be my aim. To take another example. It is part of the recognized equipment of a Montessori school that there should be a little washstand with soap and water and towels. The children are given the most minute instruction as to how the ceremony of washing and drying one's hands is best carried out. Now in the Atrium I would have this same action (of washing of hands) done over again, but with an entirely new significance. I would ask the priest to come and very carefully go through the action of the washing of the hands, as it is done before Mass, explaining to the little ones the significance of the ritual, and teaching them to say the prayers.

After that I would have them go through the action themselves, repeating at the same time the words that accompany it.

Question: And would manual work enter in here, too?

Dr. Montessori: Manual work would form an important feature of the Atrium. There would be a little carpenter's bench for the older children where they would make wooden models. At different times of the year they could make models appropriate to the particular liturgical season. Thus at Easter they could make a small cross, at Christmas a crib. It would be a good thing if a number of them joined together in making a more complicated model—such as the Temple at Jerusalem or the stable at Bethlehem. There would also be plenty of scope for weaving, clay-modeling and embroidery.

All these things would help to make the children understand the kind of life our Lord Himself lived as a child; for I would have the little ones realize that the religious life is not a thing apart from ordinary everyday life, *but one complete life which includes and takes up into itself the common things of life*. This is one of the reasons why I should like the children—as far as circumstances and climate permit—to do as we did at Barcelona, where they grew their own wheat and grapes, to obtain the bread and wine to be offered up in the Mass of their first Communion. It is a good thing, anyhow, for children to take care of plants and watch for themselves the mystery of growth. This activity takes on a still higher purpose when the materials they have helped to produce are to be offered up in the highest act of worship—to be changed into the very Body and Blood of our Lord.

I would also have the children become acquainted with the other *elements* which are used in the sacramental life of the Church—for instance, salt, oil, water, olives, incense, etc. As we did at Barcelona I would have the priest go through the ceremony of blessing the water, and the children could afterwards write out parts of the prayers, e.g., "Fill this element of water, O God, with Thy power and blessing that it may be endowed with divine grace to drive away devils."

Water indeed is such an important element in the life of the Church—being used in baptism, at the *Lavabo,* at the washing of the feet on Holy Thursday, at the blessing of the font on Holy Saturday, and in the rite of the Mass itself, as well as at other times—that I would have it much in evidence. I would have a little fountain in the garden with a pond containing fish. The children themselves would look after the fish, and I would have a little tablet near the pond—a replica of one of the ancient inscriptions from the catacombs—showing the fish as the symbol of Christianity.

Question: Where would you have your pond?

Dr. Montessori: In the cloister garden. You told me that expense was to be no object! So, adjoining the Atrium, I would have a special garden for the children. The ideal thing would be to have the school arranged like a monastery round a little cloister. The church could be on one side, the Atrium on another, and on the other two the ordinary schoolrooms. I would have statues at the end of the cloisterwalks to which the children could bring flowers. The children could play in the cloister garden, and I would like a tree in it with a little house up in the branches into which the children could climb, as they had in one school I visited in California.

In this garden I would like the children to keep as many as possible of the Evangelical Animals and Plants.

Question: What do you mean by the "evangelical" animals and plants?

Dr. Montessori: I mean the various animals and plants that play a conspicuous part in Bible history and symbolism. For instance I would like the children to have a pet lamb to remind them of the "Lamb slain from the foundation of the world." They could have a dovecot and keep doves, because of the two turtle-doves our Lady offered up at the Temple, and the dove that was sent out of the Ark and also because the dove is the symbol of the Holy Spirit. They could keep bees, too, and have some candles made with the wax their own bees had made. These could be blessed and placed on their school altar.

Nature study would form an essential element in the work of the Atrium. In my description of our work at Barcelona I have indicated the reason for this, viz., that from the observation of created things the child's mind should be raised to their Creator. As the psalmist says: "The heavens declare the glory of God and the firmament showeth His handiwork."

Question: What about such visual aids as wall charts in the classroom?

Dr. Montessori: On the walls of an ordinary Montessori school you see numbers of cards hanging up, some containing little poems, some lists of spelling examples, others the parts of speech, and so on. The children are constantly reading these and spontaneously copy them down. Similarly in the Atrium, besides the sacred pictures which I have mentioned, I would hang up a variety of cards. These would be tastefully prepared, written in beautiful script, and embellished with ornamental designs after the manner of the old monastic manuscripts. They would include such writings as:

a. Sacred mottoes, such as one sees written on the walls of churches or on the altar, e.g., "Holy, Holy, Holy!" "You are all fair, O Mary."
b. Definitions of the Sacraments.
c. The Works of Charity.
d. Acts of Faith, Hope, Charity, etc.
e. The Fruits of the Holy Spirit.
f. The Confiteor.
g. The Lord's Prayer.
h. The Hail Mary.
i. The Gloria.
j. The Apostles' Creed.

To some of these sacred inscriptions I would assign a more conspicuous place than on the wall. The *Ten Commandments*, for instance, I would have actually engraved on a slab of stone, which I would place on a little stand or lectern, specially made, so as to be just the right height for children. Next to this lectern I would have a statue of Moses—preferably a small replica of the one by Michelangelo—and behind and above it a candlestick with the seven candles.

On a similar stand, beside a statue of St. Peter, I would place the *Commandments of the Church;* and, on a third, beside a statue of Christ, the *Commandments of Our Lord.*

The children would have these writings on the wall and on the lecterns constantly before them, and at a certain stage—when they are learning to write—they would spontaneously and with great enjoyment copy them. They would keep their copies in a special folio, as they do the multiplication tables which they have themselves worked out, and would use them, like the latter, for memorizing.

Use of Models in the Atrium

Question: Would you approve of the use of little model altars for the children to learn about the Mass?

Dr. Montessori: Yes, we had them at Barcelona. I think these models may be very helpful as long as they are used in a proper way.

Question: What do you mean by a proper way?

Dr. Montessori: Well, to begin with, the model altar must never be confused in the child's mind with the real thing. The models should only be used for *learning the names of things and their uses.* They must never forget, for instance, that a real altar contains an altar-stone with some relics and that a priest could not say Mass without such a stone.

Care should also be taken that the child's preoccupation with the model altar does not degenerate into a mere game.

In the Notre Dame Montessori School at Dowanhill, Glasgow, the Sisters have a series of beautiful models, representing the various "mysteries," such as the

Annunciation, the Nativity, the Crucifixion and so on. The children take these models from the cupboards where they are kept, and place them on the floor. Then with the Montessori movable script alphabet they make up in their own words on a rug on the floor a short description of the incident portrayed. Such models would form desirable parts of the "environment" in the Atrium.

It would also be a good thing to have models of the ancient Tabernacle, the Temple of Solomon, a church, or a monastery, with a brief description written out for the children, and cards with the names on them, which the children could place, from memory, on the various parts of the models.

I think it is very important that children should be interested in the history of the Church. I would have little stories and pictures especially composed revealing the characteristics of the early Church—its simplicity, its fervor and its heroism. I have a great admiration for the work of one of the Benedictine Fathers in Rome. This priest takes the boys under his charge to the catacombs and explains to them how they were used by the early Christians. He goes further than this, for he actually celebrates Mass there, as was done in the early Church, and is assisted by his boys. We should do everything we can to revive the spirit of those early times.

As in those times, I would have the children follow as far as possible the actual ceremony of the Mass, and not content themselves with reading special books of devotions. The latter may be very good in themselves, but they can never take the place of the Mass itself.

Question: Would the children have any special clothes associated with the Atrium?

Dr. Montessori: In an ordinary Montessori school the children—when they come into the school—very often put on little smocks or pinafores to work in. I would have the same in the Atrium, but especially designed costumes. Some would be red, to commemorate the martyrs; others white for purity; and others green, which is the commonest liturgical color. The little girls would wear a small veil like a Spanish mantilla; and the little boys would have a cowl attached to the top of their smocks at the back. On the shoulders of each of these garments would be worked a cross to symbolize that the Christian must carry his cross—big or little as the case may be—in his daily life. For even the children have their crosses to bear, sometimes much heavier than we imagine.

Thus it will be seen that the work of the Atrium would be a much broader thing than merely "teaching the child his catechism"—often with the avowed aim of making a good impression on the diocesan inspector, or the bishop! It will rather be a life complete in itself, something which will affect the children at all points. It will be like a surrounding and pervading atmosphere in which they will live and move and have their being.

The whole trend of modern psychological research is to emphasize the permanent effect, for good or ill, of impressions in early childhood. How could these little ones, therefore, better prepare themselves for the struggle against the paganism of today and tomorrow than by being— in these formative years—*Bambini viventi nella Chiesa*—Little children living in the Church?

CHAPTER FOUR

THE SPIRITUAL TRAINING OF A TEACHER

[5]"Though all ought to possess all the virtues, yet all are not equally bound to exercise them; but each ought to practice, in a more particular manner, those virtues which are most requisite for the state of life to which he is called."

INTRODUCTION TO THE DEVOUT
LIFE, (PART III, CHAPTER I),
ST. FRANCIS DE SALES

A teacher must not imagine that he can prepare himself for his vocation simply by acquiring knowledge and culture. Above all else he must cultivate within himself a proper attitude toward the moral order. Of vital importance in this preparation is the way in which we regard a child. But our subject must not be approached from its external aspect only—as if we were concerned merely with a theoretical knowledge about the nature of a child and methods of instructing and correcting him.

Here we must insist on the fact that an instructor must be prepared *inwardly* and must consider his own character

---

[5] The substance of this chapter, and of the one following it, is taken from two courses of lectures given by Montessori—one at Cambridge in 1928, and the other at the Convent of the Assumption, Kensington Sq., London W. 8, in 1930.

methodically with a view to discovering any defects within himself which might prove obstacles in his treatment of the child. To discover defects that are already rooted in the conscience, some help will be required, *some instruction.* Thus, for instance, if we want to know what is at the back of our eye, we must get somebody else to look and tell us. In this sense the teacher must be *initiated* into her inward preparation. She is too much occupied with "the wicked tendencies of the child," and "how to correct its naughtiness," and "actions dangerous to the soul, caused by the remnants of original sin which are in the child," etc.

Instead of this she should begin by looking for her own bad tendencies and defects—"First take out the beam that is in your own eye, and *then* look for the mote in the eye of the child." This inward preparation is not concerned with "seeking one's own perfection" after the manner of those who enter the religious state. It is not necessary to become perfect and free from every weakness in order to be a teacher. A person who is continually preoccupied in trying to improve his "inward life" is probably unconscious of those defects which make him incapable of understanding a child. And that is why it is so necessary to be properly directed and prepared to be a teacher of little children.

We have within our souls numerous bad tendencies which develop like weeds in a meadow, the result of original sin. These tendencies are manifold; let us say they can be summed up in seven groups: the seven deadly sins. A child is more or less free from sin. Not only is a child, compared with ourselves, purer, but he has certain pure, occult, and mysterious qualities, generally invisible to adults, in which however we must faithfully believe because our Lord spoke of them with such clearness and insistence that all the evangelists wrote, "Except ye be converted and become as little children, ye shall not enter into the kingdom of heaven."

A teacher must be able to see the child as Jesus saw him. A teacher is one who can rid himself of all the obstacles which make him unable to understand a child; he is not merely a person who is always trying to improve himself. Our instruction to teachers consists in pointing out to them which states of mind need correction, just as a doctor would diagnose a definite and particular illness from which a human organism is suffering or in danger. Here, then, is *positive* help: "The moral defect which arises in us and prevents our understanding a child is *anger.*"

And, since no moral defect acts alone, but is always accompanied by, or combined with, other defects—just as Eve was joined by Adam as soon as sin made its first inroad— so anger is mixed up with another moral disorder, which appears less ignoble and is therefore the more diabolical: pride.

Our bad tendencies may be corrected in two ways: an interior one which consists in the struggle of the individual who, clearly and intelligently recognizing his own defects, voluntarily tries to overcome them with all his strength and purge himself of them with the help of God's grace.

The other is a social corrective which is to be found in the external environment We might point out how the resistance of earthly things, opposed as they are to any outward manifestation of our bad tendencies, must arrest their development. External opposition has considerable influence. It is, one might say, the chief reminder of the existence within us of any moral defect, and an external reminder which leads us in some cases to think about our inward state and then actively to set about our inward purification, if we really wish for it.

Let us consider these deadly sins: our pride is modified by the opinion of others; our avarice, by the material circumstances of life; anger, by the attitude of those stronger than ourselves; sloth, by the necessity of working for our living; luxurious habits, by social customs; gluttony, by the limited possibilities of procuring superfluous things; jealousy, by the wish to appear dignified. There is, no doubt, behind the above conditions, the desire of the individual to overcome his faults. But those external circumstances are a definite and continuous reminder which is quite salutary. In short, social control affords great support to the moral equilibrium of our personality.

However, while conforming to these social codes we do not feel ourselves pure in the sight of God. But although our souls conform willingly to the necessity of correcting the fault which we ourselves have recognized, they adapt themselves with difficulty to the rest of the process —the humiliating one of being controlled by others. We feel even more humiliated by the fact of having to give in than by actually having done wrong. When we are made to restrain ourselves, and there is no other way out, our instinct of worldly dignity induces us to make it appear that we have ourselves chosen what was really inevitable.

The small deception of saying, "I do not like it," about something which we cannot have is one of the most common moral traits. We resist resistance with a small deception, and so enter a battlefield rather than the road to perfection. And, as in every struggle, we shall soon feel the need of organized fighting. Individual deeds are strengthened by becoming collective. People who have the same defect, before giving in to the external causes which would go against them, are led instinctively to triumph over these by the strength of union.

The weaker the external things which are opposed to our

defects, the more time and leisure we have for construction of our camouflage and fortifications. If we penetrate a little further into these ideas we shall come to the conclusion that our vices are more fixed than we thought, and that the devil can easily insinuate himself into our subconsciousness by suggesting that we should hide our real selves from our outward selves. This defense, not of our lives but of our evil tendencies, is the mask which we readily put on, calling it "necessity," "duty," "general advantage," etc., so it becomes daily more difficult to free ourselves from this sort of thing. Confusion arises from the fact that we are now convinced that what our conscience once suggested to us was really false, is now true.

And now the teacher, or whoever wishes to educate children, must be purged of those errors which would place her in a false position with regard to children. She must realize clearly what is her prevailing defect; and by this we refer to more than one single defect—to a combination of disorders which are allied to one another—pride and anger.

Anger is one of those failings held in check by the determined reaction of others. It is one of the things that proves how difficult it is for one man to be subjugated by another. Therefore he is a prisoner when he meets a really strong person. A man is ashamed of showing anger before others because he at once sees himself in a humiliating position; that of having to retire by force.

It is therefore a real relief to be able to mix with people who are incapable of defending themselves or understanding; people who believe everything as children do. Children not only forget our offenses immediately but feel themselves guilty of everything of which we accuse them.

The teacher is here invited to reflect carefully on the serious effects of such a state of things on the life of a child. A child's understanding would not see through the deception; but his spirit feels it, and is oppressed and often warped by it. Then the childish reactions appear which really represent an unconscious self-defense. Timidity, deceit, caprice, the frequent weeping, which they seem to justify, night fears, any form of exaggerated fear—and similar obscure things— represent the unconscious state of defense of a little child who has not yet sufficient reasoning power to understand the real conditions of its contacts with adults.

On the other hand, anger does not necessarily imply physical violence. From the crude and primitive impulse which is generally understood by this word, complex manifestations may be developed. A psychically developed person conceals and complicates his inner states of evil. Indeed, anger in its simplest form only shows itself as a reaction to some open resistance on the part of the child. But in the presence of the obscure expressions of the child's mind, anger and pride are interpenetrated in a complex mass, assuming the precise, tranquil and respectable form which is called tyranny.

An oppression which is not disputed places the tyrannous person in an impregnable stronghold of authority and recognized rights. Just because he is an adult makes him right to the child. To discuss this question would be to make an attack on a state of sovereignty which is recognized and sacrosanct. In the society of adults, a tyrant used to be recognized as the elect of God. But to the child a grown-up person represents God Himself. It is beyond discussion; in fact the only person who could discuss it is the child, and he remains silent. He accommodates himself to everything, believes everything, pardons everything. When he is punished he does not try to justify himself, and willingly asks the pardon of any angry person, forgetting to inquire how he has given offense.

Sometimes, too, the child will do something to defend himself. This defense is hardly ever a direct reply to the act of an adult, but a vital defense of its own "psychic" integrity, or the reaction of a repressed spirit.

It is only when the child is growing up that he begins to direct his defense with discernment against tyranny; but then the adult finds reasons to justify himself by entrenching himself more and more behind his camouflages. Sometimes he even succeeds in convincing the child that it is for his good that the teacher becomes a tyrant.

"Respect" is paid only by one side; the weak respects the strong. An offense on the part of the teacher is legitimate; he can judge the child unfavorably, openly speak ill of him, even go so far as to strike him. The needs of the child are directed and suppressed by the teacher at will, and any protest on the part of the child is an insubordination which it would be dangerous to tolerate.

Just as some people have succeeded in believing that everything will be secured to them through the benevolence of their sovereign, so children believe that they owe everything to the benignity of the teacher. Or, rather, it is the teacher who believes it—who in his pride has convinced himself that he has created everything that is in the child; *he* makes him intelligent, learned, good, religious. That is to say, it is *he* who has prepared the way necessary to put the child in communication with his surroundings, with man and with God. This is a fatiguing mission. (The renunciation of the tyrant completes the tyrant. There never yet was a tyrant who confessed to having sacrificed his subjects.)

What our method asks of a teacher as preparation is that she should examine herself, and purge herself of the defect of tyranny, eradicating the ancient mixture of pride and anger with which her heart is unconsciously encrusted. She must cast off pride and anger and—first of all—become humble before she can put on charity. That is the state of mind which she must attain. This is the central point of equilibrium without which it is impossible to advance. This is the inward "preparation," the point of departure and arrival.

This does not imply that we should approve of everything the child does, or abstain from criticizing him, or do nothing to help the development of his intelligence and feelings. On the contrary, we must never forget that the whole point of the argument is to educate, to become the real masters (*maestri*) of the child.

What is called for is an act of humility. We must pluck from our hearts a rooted prejudice, just as the priest before ascending to the altar recites his *Confiteor*. Only thus can it be done.

The teacher who is preparing himself inwardly by putting on charity differs from a person who is just trying in a general way to acquire that sublime quality. Charity, as described by St. Paul, includes all the highest perfections of Christianity. But the teacher must study that part of charity which is indispensable for his particular mission. Here, too, he needs a guide to direct him toward these special points.

One might describe the kind of charity necessary to a teacher as a searchlight which concentrates its light and turns it on a distant object.

It is obvious that a religious soul who is constantly seeking for perfection, and consequently for charity, will more easily direct his searchlight so as to illuminate the child mind. Yet it is true that the most vigilant and enlightened soul, with his light spread over everything, might yet pass near a child without having the special outlook of a teacher.

The charity which helps people to become teachers of little

children is that which shows itself in the child, the goodness which the child itself succeeds in showing. Teachers and all those engaged in education, however, are more inclined to see evil, so that they may check it at once in the most effective and thorough way. It seems rather as if in that alone consisted all the essentials of a moral education. In this way the roots of good which are beginning to sprout in the children's soul may remain unrecognized and denied.

An observant person might often believe that it was he who had sowed the seed of good in the child's soul, and be blind to many delicate and childlike expressions of goodness, just as one who suffers from daltonism is blind to certain colors.

A sensibility capable of seeing good wherever it may be found, even if it is something quite small and hidden away, is allied to the perfect love of which our Master, Christ, was the exemplar. And that love, which lights up everything, we call "charity."

We must not confuse this kind of charity with vague forms of optimism. It does not make us regard all existing things as good, but only what is really good and on that account, to be clearly distinguished from evil. Thus the eye of a great artist recognizes at once a really precious object, even if it is small and mixed with many ugly and vulgar things; while, on the contrary, an uneducated person, insensitive to beauty, might regard the ugly things as pleasing, and be blind to the beauties of a real work of art.

The kind of goodness to which everything seems good, and evil nonexistent, is, therefore, something totally different from the charity which is needed in good teachers of the young.

The Wheat Field—An Illustration

In a field of ripe wheat the ears seem at first sight all alike, but on looking carefully one notices several kinds and, especially, that some are more beautiful than others—they are full, and bent with their weight. The grain of these, when ground, not only gives more flour, but a very white flour, especially rich in nutritive value. Not only that, but these ears of superior quality are almost immune from the diseases which are liable to attack the weak and inferior wheat.

Farmers have only recently become aware of these important facts, and have busied themselves in selecting the better kinds of grain and discarding the inferior, with a view to cultivating only the best kind in their fields.

The result, however, cannot be attained as easily as appears at first sight, for the better grain requires more care to make it grow; and that is the reason why so little of this variety can be found in ordinary fields.

To make the kind of wheat with heavy ears flourish, the earth must be intensively cultivated with special fertilizer; and only by preparing a new and perfect medium can intensive culture succeed in getting a field uniformly covered with this valuable and wonderful grain. If the intensive care of the field is the least neglected, the beautiful ears begin to dwindle and get lighter in weight and finally become diseased.

"This is degeneration," thought the agriculturists who had sown the field entirely with selected seed. But the biologists, led by de Vries ("The Theory of Mutations") have given an "experimental" explanation of the above phenomenon. It was not a case of "degeneration." Grains of the poorer quality had remained hidden in the earth, and had not sprouted because the ground was intensively fertilized in such a way as to vitalize the large seeds which, so nourished, prevent the growth of the inferior seeds. These, smothered by the stronger kind, remained concealed and latent, with no room to germinate.

It is well known how wheat can survive; even if it does not sprout properly it still remains alive and capable of germination. Thus, when the cultivation of the ground was neglected, it happened that the large grains, which required a great deal of special nourishment, could not grow, while the old seed, which did not need so much, grew quite easily. And the more the grower neglected the land, the more the inferior seed, poor and sickly, found its chance of living and springing up. The grower who had sown his seed entirely with the strong-growing grains could not explain the appearance of so many kinds of inferior wheat. But the bad seed which was sown had persisted, awaiting its opportunity. Superior grain cannot live poorly, it needs a great deal to make it grow. Thus we see that it is not sufficient to have good seed without taking care of its environment. Good seed and bad seed are always there; the cultivation of the good is more difficult, but when it finds the conditions favorable it overcomes the bad and gives prodigious results.

Want of care does not leave the field barren, for, in the place left empty by a heavy ear, light ears spring up. Good conquers evil or evil conquers good. The field is always full either with good growth or bad.

If good things are not nourished we suffer not only from the lack of them but also from the presence of worse things.

In a neglected field, or in one short of water, there is not only the absence of good tender grass, but also the presence of rank weeds, intruding all the more where the vital conditions for good grass are wanting.

It happens also with the soul somewhat as it happens with

the wheat field and the meadow. Progress in agriculture began with discovering and studying the best ears, and then solved the problem by procuring the necessary things for their cultivation. There will not be a good harvest merely by exterminating the inferior plants. The surest way of keeping down the bad seed is to encourage the growth of the good.

The sudden extermination of evil is not a thing to be recommended. This is clearly taught by our Divine Master; it is better to let tares also grow, than to destroy the good grain along with them. The key to the problem is, therefore, not to destroy evil but to cultivate good.

CHAPTER FIVE

TEACHING RELIGION TO YOUNG CHILDREN

For the catholic, the question of *what* to teach in religion does not really arise. It is our duty as parents and teachers to pass on to the next generation the "Deposit of Faith" which has been handed down through the centuries by the Church. Our problem therefore is not so much a question of *what* to teach as of *how* and *when*.

Religion as Part of a Life which Unfolds Itself

In many Catholic schools religious instruction is regarded as one subject on the curriculum among others. Usually it is a collective lesson; and the teacher follows a definite religious syllabus drawn up by the ecclesiastical authorities. It is the teacher's duty to expound certain truths, which are embodied in the catechism answers which have to be learned by heart—often against the date fixed for the diocesan inspection.

Our view of the matter is somewhat different. Not that we object to collective lessons, as such; but we regard them as part of a wider whole. Still less do we object to a religious syllabus outlining what is necessary for the children to learn.

It is rather our whole attitude to the child and our conception as to the best way of teaching him, that is different.

We have defined education as "an aid to life"; and a Montessori school might be defined *as a Prepared Environment in which children can live their own lives according to the laws of their development.*

From this point of view, therefore, it seems to us that the teaching of religion should, as far as possible, form a spontaneous and integral part of the child's mental and spiritual life, as it unfolds itself from hour to hour and day to day, in the free social and intellectual environment in which he finds himself.

The Adult May Become an Obstacle Rather than a Help

Long experience has shown us that the adult, however sincere and willing, may become an obstacle to the child's mental and spiritual development, by not understanding—and therefore not respecting—the laws of his development referred to above. This happens particularly when the adult imagines that it his duty to mold the intelligence and the soul of the child by the direct and forceful impact of his own dominating personality. Such a teacher, when it comes to the question of religious teaching and training, is inclined to assume the attitude of one who should say: "Leave it to me; I am the destined individual by, and through whom, everything must come: I will supply all that is necessary for the child's enlightenment and spiritual growth."

The difference I am trying to put before you may be illustrated by the well-known incident in the Gospels—the one in which our Lord reproves His disciples, saying, "Suffer the little children to come unto Me. . . ." This is often interpreted to mean: *"Lead* the little children to Me." But the words of the Gospel suggest a different meaning: "Permit the little children to come to Me." It becomes therefore a question of the attitude of the adult toward the children. The adult becomes an obstacle when he tries to do himself what should be done by the child, to do what in fact *can* only be done by the child. On hearing this some adults—misunderstanding what I am trying to explain—might exclaim: "Very well then, we won't teach the child anything! Let him come to God by himself!"

"Help Me to Help Myself

To act in this way would of course be to *abandon* the child, not help him. *The important thing for us to realize is that we are helping a child who has a principle within him.* There exists in fact in the child an inner creative force which is much stronger than we usually realize. Our aim therefore should be to help him to help himself. The deepest longing of the child's soul—if he could only articulate it—would be expressed in just this way: "Help me to help myself." We must learn how to assist the child in such a way that he can act independently of us; and in so doing create within himself new knowledge and new power. This implies that we must seek the limits of our help in accordance with the golden maxim *"Every useless aid arrests development."* In short our aim is a collaboration between the child and an adult, who gives the minimum assistance to enable the child to work spontaneously and creatively on his own.

The Law of Sensitive Periods in Development

Generally speaking in religious education we do not sufficiently take into account the psychology of the child, i.e., *the laws* which govern his mental development. One of the most important of these is the law of sensitive periods. Put briefly this means that, as the individual develops, he passes through a succession of well-defined stages or epochs, each of which is characterized by a peculiar sensitivity to certain aspects of his environment; and a corresponding capacity to absorb them into his mental life.

A sensitive period may be compared to a ray of interest—like a searchlight coming from the child's mind—which lights up certain things in the world around him with a peculiar vividness and fascination. While it is there it enables him to absorb those things with an astonishing ease and power. But a sensitive period is a transitory phenomenon, lasting just long enough for the child to establish certain acquisitions and skills. Then it passes—never to return—giving place to another, which in its turn is succeeded by the next, and so on.

It is obvious that a knowledge of these sensitive periods will have a profound effect on the way we teach—especially upon *what* we shall teach at any given age. We must place as the basis of all instruction the fact that a child can understand different things at different ages. It is not merely a question of beginning with the simplest and most easy parts of a subject and then gradually proceeding to the more difficult. It is rather the fact that at different epochs children absorb things in different ways. The important thing is to present at any epoch those aspects of the subjects taught which correspond to it. Hence we must see to it that the child's environment should be furnished with those things which correspond to the needs and special capacities of each successive period.

The Absorbent Mind

From a study of the different ways children react under the different sensitive periods, one fact stands out with remarkable clearness, viz., that during the period up to seven the child possesses a different kind of mind from that of the adult. To take just one example, the learning of one's mother tongue. Whereas an adult sets out deliberately and with a conscious mental effort to learn a language, the small child "absorbs" it unconsciously from its environment simply by living it. Further it does it more perfectly and without fatigue. To distinguish this sort of an intelligence from that of the adult we have called it "the absorbent mind."[6]

We may divide the epoch of the absorbent mind into two sub-stages: the first, (1-3 years) in which the child's mind works unconsciously; and the second (3-6 years) in which the process of absorbing becomes increasingly self-conscious. But the essential thing, all along, is that the assimilation of knowledge is a spontaneous activity directed by the urge of the various sensitive periods through which the child passes. This reveals itself in a "love for the environment" which "burns without consuming" and builds up the personality.

The Age of Reason Succeeds the Absorbent Mind

What happens when the absorbent mind begins to wane? Another faculty then begins to assert itself—which is the reason. The child now begins to show a keen interest in the causes of things—their "inner connections" as Froebel called them. It gives him pleasure, now, to see the phenomena of the world around him held together in the bonds of reason. His intense preoccupation with the sensorial qualities of things begins to wane as his mind rises to a more intellectual level.

For centuries educationists have been aware of this change which sets in about the seventh year. In fact it has often been described as the "coming of the age of reason." This is why

---

[6] See Montessori's last great work *The Absorbent Mind.*

many educational authorities maintain that this is the right age for the child to begin school. For now he can grasp—apprehend—what we tell him. He has become teachable. In the same way—and upon the same grounds—many people think that this is also the age to begin the teaching of religion. And so catechism lessons commence.

An Unfounded Assumption

But behind this procedure lies an unfounded assumption, viz., that it is useless to begin serious religious instruction before the age of reason begins. Behind this also lies the still more fundamental assumption that the child is *incapable* of acquiring religious knowledge except on the intellectual plane.

The more one studies the nature of the absorbent mind, the more unfounded do these assumptions appear. Our whole experience for the past forty years with children under seven in all parts of the world confirms the contrary. It has been proved beyond any doubt that during the ages of 3½ to 7 years children when placed in the right conditions can, and do, absorb an immense amount of knowledge spontaneously, which includes many of the elements of culture. This is not the place to show how children in our schools, during these precious years, learn to write and read, study arithmetic, geometry, geography, history and other subjects. What concerns us here are the general principles of method by which this *self-education* is brought about, so that we can apply it to the teaching of religion.

The Importance of the "Prepared Environment"

In the first place it must be a method which enables the educator to make the fullest use of the absorbent mind so characteristic of this period. The secret of being able to do this lies in the creation of a "prepared environment" in which we place those elements of culture we wish the children to absorb. Obviously, however absorbent the child's mind may be, potentially, it cannot absorb what is not there.

The Child Learns through Movement

The next question which confronts us is: *in what form* are we to place in the prepared environment those items of knowledge which we wish the child to absorb? Shall it be in the form of books? Certainly not! For the child, at the beginning at any rate, cannot read; in fact reading is just one of the things which we wish him to learn at this epoch. Shall it be in the form of pictures? Visual aids? That will not do either: for just *looking* at things will not bring about that intense and long-continued concentration of a mind that is absorbing under the spell of a sensitive period. Neither can this absorption be brought about by the child's "hearing." We may coerce or cajole the children into sitting still and listening *ad lib, (our* lib!) but that will not suffice.

How then is the child's mind to absorb what we put into the prepared environment? The answer is *movendo-si,* literally "by moving himself," or to use the more customary phrase *"through activity."* Better still through self-activity, *Selbst-tatigkeit* as Froebel called it.

What Kind of Activity is Essential?

And now comes what is perhaps the most important question of all (especially in view of the present cult of the "activity school"). *What kind of activity?* Everyone knows that, unless children are asleep or inhibited, they are always in motion. What is there special about the kind of activity which accompanies the operation of the absorbent mind? It would be impossible to give a complete answer within the limitations imposed upon us here. All we can say, at the moment, is that it must be a form of what we call "synthetic activity," that is movement which brings into full co-operation the two main elements of the child's personality—mind and body—the intelligent, directing will on the one hand, and the co-operation of the voluntary muscular system on the other. It must be a form of sensory-motor activity by which some reality[7] in the outside world asserts its presence, acting through the "point of contact" at the "periphery" and starting the vital process of self-construction in the "center" of the child's personality.[8]

For Fixing Motor Habits

It must not be thought—during this first period of childhood (up to 7)—the Absorbent Mind is the only characteristic that stands out. There are others, too, as for instance the Sensitive Period for Order which reaches its peak at about two years. Another very important one (2½ to 5) is the child's interest in, and capacity for, perfecting bodily movements that have an intelligent aim; and thereby acquiring precise motor habits. This is the period when the appeal of the Exercise in Practical Life is at its strongest; and it is also the period marked out by nature for learning good manners—which is helped on through the Lessons of Grace and Courtesy.

Now in the share of religious practice there are certain actions, connected with worship, which one might describe

---

[7] Not make-believe.

[8] For a fuller elucidation on this question the reader is referred to Section Four (The Significance of Movement in Education) in *Maria Montessori—Her Life and Work* (pp. 208 ff).

as the good manners of the Church. These include such actions as making the Sign of the Cross, with or without holy water, genuflecting, kneeling down and standing up during a service, carrying lighted candles without spilling grease, placing flowers at the foot of a statue and so on. Such actions and many similar ones should be taught to the children at this early epoch for at this time these have a very special appeal. At this stage every detail of an action is of great interest to them. They are as particular in having them done correctly as a master of ceremonies. This will not be the case a year or two later, when the Sensitive Period has passed.

In this same sensory-motor period (as it is sometimes called), the child also has a special interest in the sensorial qualities of things—their colors, size, texture, shape, sounds, and so forth. Now the liturgy of the Catholic Church is rich in the lavish use of material aids to religion at this sensorial level—colored vestments, incense, dignified and stately actions, beautiful forms, statues, pictorial representations, resplendent lights and so forth. It is precisely during this sensory-motor period—well before the age of reason sets in—that these things exert the most powerful fascination. In what particular ways we can make use of this interest at this age in practice will become clearer in chapter twelve in which we shall describe the Atrium—the specially prepared environment for the teaching of religion.

A Short Summary

Meanwhile let us conclude this chapter with a resumé of some of the main points discussed in it.

1. As Catholic teachers our main problem is not so much *what to* to teach, as *how*.
2. Education is an "aid to life."

3. Religious education is therefore to be looked upon not so much as a school subject as an aid to spiritual life which unfolds of itself. It is a religious person we are aiming at rather than one who has received certain instructions.

4. We place at the center therefore the personality of the child.

5. This personality develops in accordance with certain interior laws which have been revealed to us by the children themselves working freely and spontaneously in our schools.

6. It is essential that we should acquaint ourselves with these laws (especially the Law of Sensitive Periods and of the Absorbent Mind) and adapt our whole approach to the child in accordance with them.

7. We can best help the child—during these pre-reason periods—*indirectly;* by placing him in a Prepared Environment in which we have provided those elements of knowledge which we wish him to absorb—and up to a point this is also true of religious knowledge.

8. This spontaneous absorption of knowledge—in the sensory-motor period—is always accompanied by an activity which unites hand and brain, body and mind.

9. The Prepared Environment would be useless without the Prepared Adult—the adult who understands and forms the dynamic link between the children and this environment.

10. The Directress will, of course, also give direct collective lessons, telling Bible Stories and presenting the elements of religious knowledge suitable to this age, but—

11. The Directress will also—and predominantly—direct the children, as free individuals, living their own lives,

and acquiring knowledge spontaneously through self-chosen work with the religious materials. These latter materials are to be presented to them in response to the various sensitive periods through which they are passing.

12. Such activity with religious materials is not confined to any particular school "period." A child is free to work with them all morning if he is so minded, just as—on another day—he might concentrate for an equally long time on arithmetic, history or grammar. In this way religion (like the other subjects) becomes an aid to a life which develops freely and spontaneously from moment to moment and day to day.

PART TWO

CHAPTER SIX

Montessori Principles In The Light Of Scholastic Philosophy

[9]*by E. M. Standing*

Experimental psychologists have long looked upon rational psychology with a jaundiced eye, dismissing it as too theoretical. Now they are discovering that too much that is being unearthed in the laboratory and the clinic is inexplicable or fragmentary without reference to common principles; much of what Freud and Adler and Jung have to say lacks solid foundation. Many psychologists are taking a second look at the psychology that has been developed with painstaking care over the last 2,500 years.

It seems to be the fashion among psychologists of the present day to start off by decrying rational psychology as outmoded, not to say defunct. Having done this they proceed to write chapters on reason, imagination, memory, attention, etc., as if nothing had happened. As Professor Spearman remarks, "the faculties have a way of losing every battle but always

---

[9] Reprinted from *Dominicana*.

winning the war." This goes to show that there must have been something in rational psychology which was fundamentally true. It is not likely, on the face of it, that the introspective and analytical genius of so many philosophers from Aristotle to Kant should have been completely on the wrong track!

Montessori and Rational Psychology

Actually the conception of the soul according to Aristotle and the scholastics is much more in a line with Hormic philosophy than is generally supposed. For them the soul was a spiritual principle, and as such was something "simple," that is incapable of being divided into parts. And therefore, by definition, the faculties of the soul could never be separate entities but were rather modes of activity. Knowledge, will and appetite were never thought of as really separate by philosophers like Saint Thomas Aquinas. On the other hand, it needs no great introspective acumen to realize that when a person, with eyes closed, is giving himself up to the enjoyment of honeysuckle on a summer evening that the faculty of sense (smell) is occupying the spotlight of consciousness, while the knowing and willing faculties are in the background. Similarly, at some times the knowing faculty may be to the fore; and at other times, the will. To suggest, as some do, that the undeniable discoveries which have been made by modem psychologists have rendered valueless the whole of traditional psychology would be as foolish as, to quote William James, "to empty out the baby with the bath water." *A priori*, then, we should expect to find that a method of education which was based by experiment solidly and squarely on the true nature of man would fit in with the new psychology as well as the old. And so it does.

The Human Reason

Aristotle, the greatest of the rational psychologists, defines man as a rational animal—a definition which has been endorsed by every subsequent generation. "What a piece of work is man! How noble in reason and apprehension! How like a god! How different from the 'beast that lacks discourse of reason.'" In striking contrast to many of her contemporaries Maria Montessori insists, like Shakespeare, on this unique gift of man as distinguishing him from animals. Take, for instance, this rather surprising quotation from *The Secret of Childhood*:

> The baby starts from nothing: it is an active being going forward by its own powers. Let us go straight to the point. The axis round which the internal working revolves is *reason*. Such reason must be looked upon as a natural creative function that little by little buds and develops and assumes concrete form from the image it absorbs from the environment. Here is the irresistible force, the primordial energy. Images fall at once into pattern at the service of reason. It is in the service of reason that the child first absorbs such images. . . .

or again:

> The child is passing from nothingness to a beginning. He is bringing into being that most precious gift which gives man his superiority—reason. On this road he goes forward long before his tiny feet can carry forward his body.

The Soul Informs the Body

It was the scholastic doctrine that man is a being whose very nature is a compound of two different elements, spirit and matter. He is not a pure spirit who has dropped, temporarily and by mistake, into a material world, hampered therefore by a body, and waiting for the moment when he can escape. The doctrine of the resurrection of the body clearly indicates that the true nature of man is a compound of body and soul. No *theory* with regard to the interrelation of these two elements could better express the principles behind Dr. Montessori's practice in dealing with young children. Her doctrine of the "Progressive Incarnation of Man" (not reincarnation, if you will please note!) is based precisely on this most intimate relation between the soul and the body. To quote from what we have written elsewhere: The newborn child is "incompletely incarnated." Unlike most of the higher animals which are born with a marvelously complete, but instinctive power of carrying out complicated actions (directed to instinctive ends) the newborn child is comparatively helpless. He has very limited powers of muscular co-ordination.

This apparent inferiority is however really the mark of the child's superiority. For, and this is the fundamental point on which Dr. Montessori insists and upon which all her practice is based, *man's nature consists in the perfect union of body and soul,* not the soul of the animal completely dependent on the matter of its body, but an immaterial, rational, supersensitive soul. Her observations on very small children, even before they can talk and walk, have led her to believe that the very small child is often at a disadvantage, because adults do not realize that it is a being who possesses knowing and willing faculties out of all proportion to its power of expression. Therefore, it is the duty of parent and teacher not only to foster the physical growth of the child, and help him to acquire ordered physical experience, but also to enable the child to perfect the relation between soul and body, so that the latter becomes the apt instrument and means of expression of the former. This is the reason why Dr. Montessori has introduced into her classes those original "Exercises in Practical Life" so often misunderstood by outsiders, but so beloved by the children themselves. They are many and various. They include, for example, one series of actions directed to the care of the person: washing hands, combing one's hair, cleaning shoes, etc.; another, directed to the care of the environment: dusting, sweeping, scrubbing; a third, to the "Lessons in Grace and Courtesy" and many others.

Of deep significance in connection with these is the teacher's duty in presenting to the children what Dr. Montessori aptly describes as *"The Logical Analysis of Movements."* In every complicated action, such as opening and shutting a door, there is a logical sequence of subsidiary actions which collectively make the whole, and this sequence cannot be neglected without confusion and loss of grace. For example, it is no use pulling the door toward you until you have finished turning the handle. The principle in this analysis is always the same. *The light of reason is brought to bear on these actions, transfusing them with an intelligence which relates all the parts in logical order.* These distinctions may seem trivial to us, but are not so to a child of three or four, who finds such a deep interest in them that he will repeat the actions again and again, ever more perfectly, and with a sense of increasing power. In this way the child's motor-forces are gathered together and co-ordinated toward reasonable ends, and order replaces disorder.

Relation between the Senses and Intellect

In all the Montessori sensory occupations the child is busy composing and decomposing groups of objects which form carefully graded or contrasting series. And as he arranges and rearranges them, his mind forms ever more clear notions with regard to such ideas as length, breadth, color, tone, geometric forms, and the like. This is a practical application of St. Thomas' oft-repeated dictum that the human mind knows "by composition and division." It is important to realize that the child's mind is as active during these operations as his hands.

The clearly defined images which the children derive from these graded sensory materials become to them as "keys which open up new realms in the world around them." These clearly defined images form what the scholastics called the "phantasms," from which the child's intellect derives corresponding ideas, equally clear. Those conversant with Aristotelian psychology will recognize in these examples of Montessori method a familiar principle: Nothing is in the intellect which was not first in the senses. As St. Thomas expands the notion:

> There are three degrees of the cognitive faculty. There is first the act of the corporeal organ, i.e., the sense, which knows particulars; secondly, the power, which is neither the act of the bodily organ nor conjoined with corporeal matter, and such is the intellect of angels, the object of which is form as it exists without matter; and thirdly, there is the human intellect, which stands midway between the other two, which is the form of a body, although not the act of a bodily organ ... We must therefore admit that our intellect knows material things by abstractions from phantasms; and that by material things so considered it becomes in some manner able to understand immaterial things.

No words could describe the mental processes which, to the observer, appear to be taking place in the minds of the children as they work spontaneously with the various didactic materials in the Montessori school. There are indeed moments of sudden intellectual expansion in the lives of these tiny scholars when one can almost see the "agent intellect" abstracting the "intelligible species" from those "phantasms" which the children have gained through contact with the material. These are to the children moments of pure joy (to the teacher no less so). It is the joy which accompanies the right use of a faculty; and St. Thomas remarks that what we learn with pleasure we learn better than what we learn without pleasure.

We can thus imagine two pictures in the mind's eye: one of the great St. Thomas defending Aristotle against the Platonists in the Schools of Paris; the other of Madame Montessori (six centuries later) observing the astonished revelations of her liberated children in her first school in the San Lorenzo slum at Rome. At first sight there does not seem much in common between these pictures; but on looking closer we shall find they are both doing the same thing, showing forth the true nature of man.

Learning by Discovery

Many of these sudden and joyous illuminations (they are called "Montessori Explosions" by the teachers) are the result of intellectual discoveries of numerical or other relationships. They are indeed "truths that wake to perish never," which burst like new planets into their ken.

Space forbids the multiplication of examples; but spontaneity is one of their striking and essential features. Indeed the whole Montessori Method is based, and based successfully, on the spontaneous activity of the human intellect. Hence its value as against most other systems, for as St. Thomas says: "There are two ways of acquiring knowledge. (1) by *invention* or finding out, and (2) by *discipline* or learning. *Invention* is the higher mode and *discipline* stands second."

Breaking up Truth into Simpler Parts

One of the reasons why Dr. Montessori has been so extraordinarily successful in teaching by "auto-education" (or *Invention*) arises from the clearness with which she has grasped, and the originality with which she has applied, the principle which she calls "The Analysis and Separation of Difficulties." She says, in effect, that when we present a truth to be perceived by the immature mind, and we find it beyond the power of that mind to assimilate, it is no use fretting, or coercing, or persisting in presenting that truth; we must set about analyzing it into simpler elements, and then present each of these separately. This is also the method of St. Thomas: the truth must be broken up until something is reached which the mind *sees*, i.e., until it *sees* a logical connection between subject and predicate.

The Spontaneity of the Intellect

Montessori, as we have seen, bases her method on the spontaneous activity of the human intellect. Here again she is in agreement with the scholastic principles. St. Thomas taught that "the natural inclination of man is toward knowing" and that "a faculty of itself does not err concerning its own proper object *under normal conditions*." The intellect has been created to know the truth; and if a thing is made for a certain purpose it would be a contradiction in terms to say that it could not reach its object.

The phrase *under normal conditions* is the most important point as far as the present discussion is concerned. If the Montessori child reveals an altogether unsuspected capacity for spontaneous intellectual concentration, it cannot be because its intellect is any stronger than that of the child in ordinary school. It must be because the conditions are more favorable, for, as St. Thomas observes, "if a faculty fails it fails *per accidens.*"

Liberty

It is interesting to note that Dr. Montessori, in her practical dealings with children, has by a sure instinct worked out a method which is in remarkable conformity with scholastic views regarding the nature of human liberty.

The following is a summary of the main points taken from Leo XIII's papal encyclical *Libertas Praestantissimum:*

1. Only those who have the gift of reason can have true freedom.
2. Liberty is the faculty of choosing means fitted for the end proposed.
3. Every act of true choice is preceded by an act of judgment.
4. Because of the imperfection of man's nature a law is necessary to point out the way in conformity with reason.
5. One who acts through a power outside himself is a slave.

Anyone who studies what has been written on Montessori's idea of "Liberty" with these points in view will realize how perfectly Montessori's practice with regard to freedom in the schoolroom is in conformity with these principles.

Other parallels could be mentioned between rational psychology and Montessori's ideas derived from her experience with liberated children, for instance the relation which exists or should exist between imagination and reason, and also certain further details with regard to the part played by the "agent intellect" in the formation of abstract ideas from concrete objects. But enough has been written to show that both Montessori's theory and practice fit in with what is permanent in rational psychology, as well as with the latest discoveries in the new.

CHAPTER SEVEN

Montessori and The World Situation

BY E. M. STANDING

The Catholic Church, being founded by our Lord and guided by the Holy Spirit, possesses within herself infallible standards by which she is enabled to pass judgment on the various persons, events and movements which pass across the stage of history and influence the minds of men. What is morally bad she rejects, what is good she eventually incorporates into her own life, thereby preserving it for future generations— as she preserved what was best in the ancient world after the collapse of the Roman Empire.

Every new idea, whatever the sphere of influence in which it operates, takes time to unfold the possibilities for good or evil which are latent within it. The greater the depth, power and originality of an . the wider will be the field over which, as the years pass, it makes its influence felt. It is now half a century since the Montessori idea came into the world, and people in every country read with astonishment of the almost incredible doings of those small slum children in the San Lorenzo quarter in Rome. During that period it has passed through many vicissitudes: its principles have been examined, tested, criticized, praised and attacked from almost every possible angle. Yet during all that time, as one decade succeeded to another, it developed steadily, revealing its powers of expansion, assimilation, chronic vigor, recuperation and so on—in fact all those features which Cardinal Newman in his *Development of Christian Doctrine* described as the characteristics of any vital movement. In fact, when Montessori died in 1952 she left behind her a movement more active than ever before.

From the very beginning there were discerning persons who realized that not only was there nothing contrary to Catholic teaching and philosophy in Montessori's ideas —but there actually exists a definite affinity between the psychological principles underlying the Montessori Method and those which are put into practice by the Church in her liturgy, the one operating on the natural, and the other on the supernatural plane.

Of course there were plenty of individual Catholics who thought differently. In fact there were not wanting Catholic professors of education who, without properly understanding Montessori's ideas, or even taking the trouble to see them put in practice, read into her writings all sorts of heretical tendencies. But the highest authorities in the Church knew better; and from the beginning extended their sympathy to Dr. Montessori and to her work, because they had a truer appreciation of its nature and value.

The Montessori Idea a Discovery, Not a Method

In a previous paragraph we have used the phrase 'The Montessori Method" and it is used again many times in this book. But it is necessary to point out that the use of the term Montessori *Method* should be accompanied with a certain mental qualification—one to which no one would agree more heartily than Dr. Montessori herself. It has now become clear, to those who are deeply acquainted with her work, that the essence of it is not that she has invented a new method of education, but that she has been, under Providence, the means of making an important discovery, no less than the discovery of the true nature of the child.

Strange as it may sound, this has been hidden from us for centuries under the mask of deviations due to the child's unconscious frustration at being treated in a manner which prevented the unfolding of his true nature. It is now a scientifically established fact that if small children are treated according to certain principles they manifest certain characteristics—physical, mental and moral—which are so much in advance of our usually accepted notions of how children behave that most people find them hard to believe, unless they have had the opportunity of seeing for themselves a well-run Montessori classroom.

Children so treated—that is, given a degree of liberty of choice among the many "motives of activity" in a "specially prepared environment"—show the following characteristics: love of work in preference to play; a real intellectual concentration and persistence in work; an emotional harmony and a stability which reveals itself in their calm and orderly behavior; a love of their environment and a natural disposition to keep it in order; a striking initiative and independence of action, which is however combined with a willing obedience to those in authority; an attachment to reality rather than play-acting; a respect for the rights and property of others; a harmonious social adaptation to the group in which they live and work; and—most wonderful of all—a spontaneous self-discipline; all of which must be seen in order to be believed.

Natural Virtues

These of course are natural virtues. They are as natural to all children (when treated in the right way) as it is for a dog to wag his tail when he is pleased. The order—physical, mental and moral —which is revealed by these "normalized" children is a part of the cosmic order, and is akin to that order which keeps the stars to their appointed courses and the atoms to their affinities. As Dr. Montessori put it:

> When we gaze at the stars, twinkling in the sky, ever faithfully following their orbit, so steadfast in their position, do we think "O, how good the stars are!"? No, we only say: "The stars obey the laws that govern the universe," and we add "How marvelous is the order of creation!"
>
> A form of order in nature also appears in the behavior of children. Order does not necessarily mean goodness, but perhaps it is an indispensable way to obtain it.
>
> Before we can reach the point where we are "good" we must first enter into 'the order of the laws of nature.' Then, from this level, we can raise ourselves and ascend to a super-nature where the operation of consciousness is necessary.

But because these are natural virtues we have no right to neglect or belittle them. For, while it is true, as St. Thomas says, that "the good of a single grace is higher than the natural good of the whole universe" it is also true—and on the same authority—that the fullest development of the natural faculties is the best preparation for the supernatural life since grace builds on nature, not destroying but perfecting it.

St. Thomas Aquinas says, "It is clearly a false opinion to say that with regard to the truths of faith it is completely indifferent what one thinks about created things, provided one has the right opinion about God: an error about creatures reacts in a false knowledge about God." Now children are creatures; and, if Montessori has discovered certain basic truths about their nature and the laws of their development, it is our duty as parents and educators to become acquainted with them. And this, not only for the reason given by St. Thomas, but also for the very practical reason that we can thereby best help our children to unfold the God-given potentialities within them—both natural and supernatural.

With this in mind we have devoted several chapters to the delineation of Montessori Principles. It is impossible to apply the Montessori System to the teaching of religion—or any other subject for that matter—without some knowledge of those principles, and of the manner in which they should be put into practice when dealing with children.

The Two "Poles of Humanity"

There are still many people—even among Montessori's own followers—who think that the aim of her educational work begins and ends with the development of the individual. But, as a matter of fact, the longer she lived the more vividly did she realize the immense significance of the child—or better of childhood—*as a hitherto unimplemented social factor in the building up of human society*. To her, childhood was much more than a stage through which each individual must pass on his way to becoming an adult.

Childhood is an entity in itself, with a significance of its own of equal importance to the adult stage. That is why she always insisted that we must come to look upon childhood in a new way. Just as we have, in the ecclesiastical year, two main cycles—the Christmas cycle and the Easter cycle, each complementing the other so that together they complete the full round of the Liturgical Year—so, in the building up of a complete humanity, we have an equal need of these two stages. Childhood and adulthood are the two "Poles of Humanity," both of immense significance and each complementing the other.

Montessori said that the reason all the civilizations of the past have failed is that they have been built on adult values only. Hitherto the child, as a constructive factor in civilization, has been left out; he has been, and is still *il cittadino dimenticato,* the forgotten citizen, who has never been accorded his rights; and, as a consequence, he has never been able to contribute what is his potentially to give. We see a sort of echo of this truth in the fact that in the Old Testament we have chiefly to do with adults—and their sin—whereas the New Testament begins with a Child; and the redemption of humanity is to be brought about by a new set of values comparable to those of childhood: "for of such is the kingdom of heaven."

We may in fact summarize the significance of Montessori's work as the discovery of hitherto unsuspected energies in the child, which have been placed there by the Creator for the construction of the Adult-to-be, and with him of the Society-to-be. "The child's constructive energy, alive and dynamic, has remained unknown for thousands of years, just as the men who first trod the earth knew nothing of the immense wealth hidden in its depths" *(Education for a New World,* p. 2). In other words man has discovered in this century (but as yet educators are not generally aware of it) how to liberate the unsuspected psychic energies in childhood in the realm of the spirit, just as, in this same century, man has discovered how to release the hitherto titanic energies locked up in the atom, in the realm of matter.

"Our world," says Montessori, "has been torn to pieces and is in need of reconstruction"; and to achieve that reconstruction she sees the need of two main factors, return to religion, and the intensifying of education. What she means by "the intensifying of education" is a thing so new, and so different from what we have hitherto read into that term, that we really need a new word for it lest, in using it, there should still linger in our minds ideas and prejudices which would prevent our true comprehension.

"The child is endowed with an inner power which can guide us to a more luminous future. Education should no longer be mostly imparting of knowledge, but must take a new path, seeking the release of human potentialities...for the child is the constructor of man and society.

"Education is a natural process spontaneously carried out by the human individual, and is acquired, not by listening to words, but by experience with the environment. The task of the teacher becomes that of preparing a series of 'motives of activity,' spread over a specially prepared environment, and then refraining from obtrusive interference. Human teachers can only help the great work which is being accomplished as servants help the master. Only in this way—with the help of religion as the major and closely accompanying factor—can we build up "The New World for the New Man.'"

Seeing It Steadily and Seeing It Whole

The difficulty in realizing the immense significance of Dr. Montessori's work is that it presents so many different facets, each fascinating in itself, that it is not easy to see the movement as a whole, with all its separate aspects in due proportion. One might compare it to a painting done on a very large canvas. It is easy, by getting too close to one part of it, to become so absorbed in it as to forget that it is only a detail in a larger whole. Without question such details have real value in themselves and are worthy of study, but we should never forget that they belong to a greater whole and share the inspiration of the main theme.

Now Montessori's work is on a vastly greater scale than most people realize, and this lack of perception applies to many if not most of her followers. For this reason it is fatally easy to regard it *spezzato* (as Montessori would say), i.e., broken into separate pieces. Thus, you may find Montessorians, and others, who think the whole secret of Montessori's genius lies in the creation of her wonderful Montessori materials. On the other hand, many others think that the most important aspect of her system is the liberty which she gives to the children. And incidentally many of them think, quite wrongly, it is a liberty "to do anything they like." But at the same time they do not understand that you cannot give the sort of freedom that Montessori values without a Prepared Environment.

Others again conceive that the whole essence of the matter lies just in having the Prepared Environment, but they do not realize that it is equally essential to have a properly trained directress who acts as "the dynamic link" between it and the children for whom it was prepared. Then you will find many people, especially among her followers in America, who are interested in the Montessori Method because under it children usually learn to read and write fluently by the time they are six years of age. These people are all for incorporating it, merely for that reason, into whatever national or state system of education prevails in their particular country. They are on the wrong path, because they are quite oblivious to the fact that they are attempting an impossible thing. The Montessori approach is much deeper and wider than just those parts of it that have to do with "the Three R's." It is a total approach, and it is impossible to select and apply successfully bits and pieces of it, here and there, which have to do with this or that particular subject.

It goes without saying that these different points of view reflect themselves in different ideas as to how Montessori teachers should be trained.

We perhaps ought to mention here that there are also to be found plenty of people—and this applies especially to America at the present time—who are not really interested in Montessori, except commercially. They are mere opportunists who want to cash in on the present vogue for Montessori, and hope to make a good thing financially out of running a so-called Montessori school. Many of these pseudo-Montessori schools are perfect examples of the truth of the old Latin proverb *corruptio optima pessima,* the best becomes the worst when corrupted. They exist, for a time at any rate, on the quite unauthorized use of the name of Montessori, and the lamentable ignorance of many parents as to what a true Montessori school should be.

Much nearer to the truth than any mentioned above, and therefore much more to be commended, are those who realize the immense potentialities in the Montessori Method for bringing to the light of day that deeper and higher nature which lies hidden in every child. Their aim in starting a Montessori school is buoyed up by (to use Montessori's own phrase) "a faith in a child who does not yet exist." And they apply the method with patience and devotion until the children under them shed their deviations—as a snake its discarded skin—and reveal those characteristics of the "normalized" child which have been, and still are, the educational wonder of our age.

All this is excellent and most worthy of praise, as far as it goes; but to the Catholic Montessorian it does not go far enough. For these, their final aim will not have been attained until the "natural" virtues of the normalized child have been raised to the supernatural plane, through the influence of sanctifying grace.

And here we might notice in passing, a point already mentioned—the Montessori Method forms an admirable preparation for the "Life of the Child in the Church." Quite early in her educational career Montessori herself said it was not until her method was applied to the teaching of religion that she realized it had such significance when so applied.

Seeing or Not Seeing the Child

In one way or another, Montessori was always reminding us that "it is easy to pass quite close to the child and yet not see him" and thus remain blind to his immense potentialities. In fact, according to her, mankind as a whole has never yet "seen" the child for what he is in himself—a mysterious entity, worthy of our highest consideration and reverence.

At the same time, however, she used to point out with equal conviction that in the past century or so, there have arisen, here and there in different countries, certain individuals who have—quite independently of each other—actually come to "see" the child in a new way, with a deeper understanding and appreciation.

"An important discovery," she says (and she is thinking of her own discovery of the New Child) "is never an isolated one. It occurs simultaneously in several places, through different people, who have nothing in common. When we say 'there are ideas floating in the air,' we really mean that new ideas and sentiments are taking shape in the minds of men, as if by a spontaneous energy brought into focus with the passing of time, by the phenomenon of collective growth."

Such individuals are related in a specially intimate way to what Shakespeare calls "the spirit of the wide world dreaming on things to come." After the passage, from which we have just quoted, Montessori goes on to give various examples of persons who have shown this new evaluation of the significance of childhood.

But there are also many others, whom she does not mention: and from these we note a few as further examples.

Since such insight is more a matter of intuition than of scientific reasoning, it is not surprising that one often finds the best expression of it among the poets. Wordsworth was one of the first to be impressed with childhood in this new and deeper way. Apostrophizing the child he says:

> *Thou, whose exterior semblance doth belie*
> > *Thy soul's immensity;*
> *Thou, best philosopher, who yet dost keep*
> *Thy heritage, thou eye among the blind*
> *That, deaf and silent, readst the eternal deep*
> *Haunted for ever by the eternal Mind—*
> > *Mighty Prophet! Seer blest!*
> > *On whom those truths do rest*
> *Which we are toiling all our lives to find,*
> *In darkness lost, the darkness of the grave.*

In a remarkable little book, *Such is the Kingdom*, Lord Elton remarks ". . . the essence of what Wordsworth says, is that childhood possesses mysterious powers, and that it is a period of unique significance," (p. 21). Lord Elton is himself one of those sensitive individuals referred to above; and his little volume from which we have just quoted deals almost exclusively with the "numinous significance" of childhood. On page 29 he says: "If in children more naturally than at any other age is found both the vision that can perceive the kingdom of heaven and the humility which is the key to it, we should expect childhood to possess not only a special sanctity but supreme significance."

We may mention G. K. Chesterton as another of these who have seen the child in a new way. In his *Autobiography* he says:

"What was wonderful about childhood is that anything in it was a wonder. It was not merely a world full of miracles: it was a miraculous world . . . shining with the lost light of morning."

"I have never lost the sense that this was my real life, the real beginning of what should have been a more real life, a lost experience in the land of the living."

Learning from the Child

If there is one feature more than another which distinguishes Montessori's approach to the problem of education it is that, setting on one side all preconceived theories, she was humble enough to learn from the liberated child. As she herself says, her work as the interpreter of the child was such that from it there "begins a new path wherein it will not be the professor who teaches the child but the child who teaches the professor." This is, as we have hinted above, too much for professional educationists, among whom, naturally enough, the majority still cling to theories and practices which they have followed all their lives. And the consequence is that, while they continue to discuss endlessly all manner of theories and philosophies of education in their learned colleges, the real child—the normalized child— passes by unseen through the midst of them. That is why a certain attitude of humility is a *sine qua non* for anyone brought up on the old methods, if he is to enter deeply into the spirit and practice of Montessori's ideas.

Here, again, we may notice in Wordsworth, a striking unity with Montessori's point of view. He makes it clear that we should be prepared to learn from the child—that "Mighty Prophet, seer blest"—a state of things which seemed, and still seems, ridiculous to many adults unshakably secure in their own self-sufficiency.

A Path for the Future

There is another point on which we find that Wordsworth was in a striking and prophetic unity with Montessori. How often did Montessori insist that the work of the child is profoundly different in its nature and aims from that of an adult! The work of an adult has an external aim—to build a house, or wash the dishes, rear a family, etc.—whereas the aim of the child's work is primarily an internal one, to create the man-that-is-to-be. This work no one can do for him, not even the most willing and affectionate adult; it must be done by the child himself or not at all. All that we adults can do to help is to give him the means and the opportunity to carry out the long and continuous labor of self-creation. Not even Montessori ever succeeded in putting this truth more aptly and succinctly than did Wordsworth in a line which she repeatedly quoted: "The child is the father of the man."

Humanity at the Crossroads

It is not necessary to mention that humanity today is living on the edge of a volcano which at any moment may erupt and plunge us all into an abyss of destruction too terrible to contemplate. Sixty years ago Bergson, in his presidential address to the Society of Psychical Research, pointed out that, since the rise of modern science some three hundred years ago, man's scientific energies have been largely devoted to the exploration of the laws of the physical universe about us; and as a consequence we have learned how to harness the forces of nature in a thousand different ways.

But, he continued, there has been no corresponding research into the realm of the spirit, the human psyche. And because of this there was a danger that the immense powers of nature in the realm of matter might eventually get out of man's control—a danger dramatically foreshadowed, about the same time, in Karl Kapek's great play *R.U.R.* in which the Robots, created by man, rose up in rebellion against him to destroy him. How true was Kapek's prophetic insight we have since come to realize—only too painfully—in the awful and ever-present threat of the nuclear bomb.

A few years before her death, in *The Formation of Man*, Montessori wrote:

> It is commonplace to assert that there exists a lack of balance between the miraculous progress of his environment and the arrest of development suffered by man himself . . .

> We might compare the advance of outer and material progress to that of a powerful nation which invades and crushes a weaker one and, as always happens in barbaric warfare, the vanquished is enslaved by his own environment because he has remained weak in comparison with the environment . . . Never before did human helplessness reach that extreme point witnessed in our days.

Again referring to applied forces of nature which have got out of hand, she says:

The other day a young baker, who worked in a big mechanical bakery, had his hand caught between the wheels, which then entrapped his whole body and reduced it to a pulp. Is that not a symbol of the conditions in which mankind languishes, unconsciously, a victim of its environment?

This environment can be compared to that colossal engine which can produce fabulous quantities of food, and the workman entrapped represents our unwary and imprudent humanity which is grabbed and crushed by what should give it abundance.

Reconstruction and Destruction Meet

Happily there is a brighter side to the picture; and humanity has not been abandoned by its Creator to an *inevitable* annihilation. Though it is true that there have never been let loose such terrible forces of destruction as threaten us today, it is also true that in this same century, which has witnessed the two most terrible wars in history, there has come into existence a new understanding of the child and his potentialities. We have actually witnessed the liberation of spiritual energies in childhood which can be directed into constructive channels, and so help to save humanity from the doom which threatens it. "This," says Montessori, "is no coincidence but a direct ordering of Providence, one of those happenings linked up with the Spirit which often ordains and directs events in contrast to the ways of human logic. Destruction and reconstruction, war and peace, must meet each other when one epoch comes to an end and another begins" (Lecture on *Civilization and the Child*).

It would seem that there was a Divine Providence working to bring about those first revelations of the spiritual energies in the souls of children, in the first *Casa dei Bambini* in Rome in 1907. Significant in this context is the following extract from Montessori's own account of it in the *Secret of Childhood*. Recalling those first miraculous months "when we seemed to be living in a fairy tale," she says, "how often did I not reprove the children's teacher when she told me of the (wonderful) things the children had done of themselves. 'The only thing that impresses me' I would reply 'is the truth.' And I remember that the teacher, without taking offense and often moved to tears, replied 'You are right! When I see such things I think it must be the holy angels who are inspiring the children.'"

Christianity, not Humanitarianism

To avoid giving a distorted impression it must be emphasized again that, though the liberation of the constructive psychic energies in the normalized child has given us a new hope and a new power for the creation of a better humanity, we must not delude ourselves into thinking that they will be sufficient by themselves. That would be a humanitarian point of view. After all it still remains true that we are a fallen race; and that humanity can no more raise itself to a supernatural level by its own efforts than a man can lift himself up by his own bootstraps. Religion must always remain the prime factor in bringing about a renovation of human society—religion, first and always.

This would seem a truism to Christians of whatever denomination. But what has not been so generally recognized—and this goes for Catholics as well as others—is that in the past the beneficial effects of the efforts to teach religion have been limited by a lack of understanding of the *natural* goodness which is latent in all children. The Fall, as every Catholic admits, was a terrible tragedy; but we do not believe—and act—on the supposition, that human nature was *completely* corrupted. Montessori's work has made it clear to all "who have eyes to see" that even in spite of the moral disorder brought about by original sin, there still remains in human nature a great potentiality for goodness. This natural goodness which reveals itself in normalized children is a part of the universal order, akin to that which keeps the stars in their courses.

We pause only for a moment to underline the fact that whenever religion has been taught to children without a practical understanding of the relationship between natural and supernatural goodness, it has—apart from divine intervention—fallen short of its fullest possible effect. This is only another way of stating the truth of Montessori's remark that "to lift humanity out of its present predicament we need two factors—religion *and* an 'intensified education.' "

Need for a Precise Vocabulary of Education

Montessori used to complain at times that her main difficulty in trying to get her ideas across was that she was obliged to use words in current circulation, "because there are no others"; but very often these failed to convey her full meaning. "What we really need," she would say, "is a new vocabulary." Noted above we saw how different is her meaning of the word "work" when applied to the child or to the adult. In the same way, when Montessori says that we need "an intensified" education (along with religion) to bring about the reconstruction of society; or when she says "education is the armament of Peace," she is not using the word "education" at all with the same connotation that we usually give it. "We must realize," she says, "that the problem of reconstruction is not confined to schools as they are conceived today, and is not concerned with methods of education more or less practical, more or less philosophical. . . . We need a scientific inquiry into human personality, and we have before us in the child a psychic entity of immense magnitude, a veritable world-power if rightly used." *(Education for a New World)*

If salvation and help are to come, it is from the child, since the child is the constructor of man. . . . Education should no longer be primarily concerned with the imparting of knowledge, but must take a new path, seeking the release of human potentialities. . . . And this reconstruction requires the elaboration of a 'science of the human spirit' ... It is patient work, an endeavor based on research to which thousands of people, devoted to this aim, must contribute.

But you may say: There is nothing new in this; there are thousands of people doing educational research today, piling up statistics of all sorts. Granted! but there is a profound difference—a difference so great that it cannot be exaggerated, cannot even be conceived by the majority of educationists today.

To explain this properly would need several pages, but—trying to put it in the briefest terms—we can say that the overwhelming volume of educational research going on today is, by comparison, of little or no value, *because it is based on the study of deviated children.* And this is bound to be the case until, and unless, those who are making the research base their conclusions on the observation of normalized children. To build up volumes of research and statistics based on the behavior of *deviated* children will not help us in this new science of the study of man—of normalized man. It is not at all easy for teachers and professors of education to understand (and harder still for them to admit it if they do) that this endless research on behavior of deviated children is as futile as trying to understand the true behavior of a rational being such as man by observing the instinctive behavior of rats in a cage.

The Search for Normality in True Development

The revelation of the characteristics of normalized children has opened up an entire new world of educational research—its aim is to discover, at each succeeding stage in the individual's development, the characteristic of normality that belongs to it. In other words its aim *is to discover* that stronger, better organized, more harmonious, more intelligent, more spontaneously industrious, more socially adapted personalities will be revealed at each stage of development by allowing children to live freely in a specially prepared environment—or rather in a successive series of such prepared environments, corresponding to the well-known stages in human development. "Education must proceed upon a path lit up by these revelations, just as common medicine is based on the *vis medicatrix naturae,* on the curative forces already existing in nature, and as hygiene is based on the natural functions of the body. To assist life— that is the first and fundamental principle."

Walls of Prejudice

I may affirm that the revelations of the child are not at all difficult to obtain, the real difficulty lies in the adult's old prejudices concerning him. It lies in the total lack of understanding, and in the veil, which an arbitrary form of education based only on human reasoning and still more on the unconscious egotism of man and his pride as a dominator have been weaving, so that the values of wise nature are hidden. . . .

Another form of prejudice was the conclusion of those scientists—who had never studied and lived with normalized children—that the mental faculties of children under five years of age are impermeable to any form of culture. Thus, in the name of science, a kind of tombstone was placed over our experiments.

And yet the fact of the existence and nature of normalized children can be verified by anyone who will take the trouble to look for them in any well-run Montessori class. The mental attitude of many of these teachers and professors reminds one of the story of the man who, at the zoo, saw a giraffe for the first time, and exclaimed, "I don't believe it."

Why was it that the Montessori Movement which made such a stir in the United States about 50 years ago disappeared after a brilliant start? So completely was this so that a Catholic publisher, in returning a manuscript on the Life of Montessori, remarked that Montessori in this country was just a name in the past history of education, and had no present interest or significance. The answer is that the high and mighty in the sphere of education never really understood its real import. They did not recognize the Montessori Method as an entirely new and total approach to the whole question of education, but merely regarded it as a newfangled way of teaching reading and writing. If they did anything at all about it, they tried to fit it into the already fixed and established national systems of education. In general one could say about it what G. K. Chesterton once said about Christianity: "The Christian ideal has not been tried and found wanting. It has been found difficult and left untried."

When the professional educators read the account of the "explosion into writing" and the other wonderful things that happened in Montessori schools, they could not get away from the idea that all these things happened because of Montessori's unusual personality and as a result of a new method she had invented.

She herself says: "They thought it was I who had solved the problem. The mentality of these people could not conceive that the nature of childhood can offer a solution to a problem we adults cannot solve. . . . The correct thing to have said in the face of such facts would have been, 'Let us study these phenomena, let us work together in order to penetrate into the secret of the human psyche.' But it was impossible for them to understand that from the depths of the child's soul we can draw something new, something useful to all of us, some light that would clarify the obscure causes of human behavior. . . .

"Meanwhile many people said to me 'You do not realize what you have achieved! You are not aware of the great work you have done.' They insisted on thinking that *I* was the cause. When I continued, year after year, pointing to the child and his wonderful powers they looked at me instead, as at an educator and founder of a new method. ... It was impossible for them to accept simply the evidence of the facts. The facts, in their opinion, had to be some adult's achievement: somebody had either to produce them or imagine them."

What about the Future of Montessori in the US.A.?

When people ask—as they often do—what do you think are the future prospects of the Montessori Movement in the United States (or any other country), there is no certain answer. It depends. There will be nothing automatic either about its acceptance or rejection. When our Lord sent His disciples out into all the different parts of the world to preach the Gospel, who could have prophesied that the good seed would grow best in some European countries, and make no corresponding headway elsewhere? There is a real danger that the Montessori Movement may fizzle out in the United States, as it did 50 years ago—"found difficult and left untried."

Montessori and the World Situation

Dark and ominous as is the world situation today, with its threat of an indescribably dreadful doom, it is not without gleams of that hope "which springs eternal." In every country there are still millions of people who think that somehow or other, something may happen—some movement arise—which will save humanity. In every country there are individuals who have seen a new vision of the significance of childhood and its potentialities for the betterment of society. And now as though to define it more and more clearly, to point out the way has come Montessori with her discovery of the "normalized child," who is no longer a vague hope but a verifiable scientific fact. In every civilized country there are groups of individuals who, having seen for themselves these new children, see in them the first step toward the betterment of society. They now share Montessori's belief in the further implementation of the "human potential."

Although Montessori never doubted the immense potentialities for social reconstruction latent in childhood, which could be made actual by her "intensified education," the later years of her life were rather overshadowed by a sense of frustration at the slow progress made in the dissemination and acceptance of her ideas. She realized that this was due, more than to anything else, to the "walls of prejudice," which rose up as obstacles to the understanding and practice of her principles.

Wanted—A New Religious Order

In one of the last conversations which the present writer had with Dr. Montessori—in 1950, two years before her death—this subject came up for discussion; and the *Dottoressa* expressed herself along the following lines. She pointed out that in the history of European civilization a remarkable phenomenon has repeated itself in different centuries. When in any particular epoch there arises in human society some universal need, accompanied by a universal longing (conscious or unconscious) to have it met, then we find that, from the heart of the Catholic Church, there arises some new spiritual movement in response to it. In His wisdom and infinite love the Almighty raises up certain individuals, or groups of individuals, who start a new movement, generally in the form of a religious order.

Such was the monastic movement in the sixth century started by St. Benedict and carried on through the centuries in monastic centers throughout Europe. Again the Crusades came into existence in answer to a universally felt desire to rescue and preserve the Holy Places from the Saracens. More successful, because more spiritual in their methods, were the two great movements started in the 13th century by those spiritual geniuses, St. Francis and St. Dominic. The Mendicant Orders, with surprising suddenness, brought their message of hope and consolation and renewed spiritual life into every city, town and village. Three centuries later saw the rise of another great spiritual movement—the Society of Jesus—whose members form the popes' wonderfully trained and disciplined "shock troops." They brought—as they still do—the light of reason and sanity, inspired by grace, to bear upon the many and various intellectual problems which everywhere disturbed sincere persons in a world confused by the spread of false doctrine.

"In truth," said Montessori, "what we need is a new religious order. Here am I, and I have been working all my life for the rights of the child, for the recognition of childhood as 'the Other Pole of Humanity.' For 50 years I have been doing this, and look how little really has been accomplished. An individual working alone can be compared to a man digging by himself in a field whereas the work of a religious Order, by comparison, is like that accomplished by a bulldozer."

The Aims of the New Order

The immediate work of the Order would be to make known Montessori's great discovery of the characteristics of normalized children; and it would do this in the most practical way by setting up schools in every country where the "New Children" could be seen in actual being. ("It has always been the children, in the last analysis, who have propagated my method.")

In such an Order, in which scientific research and training would go hand in hand with complete dedication to spiritual ends, there would not be the danger of an undue emphasis being placed on this or that separate aspect of the work, to the exclusion of others, resulting in a lopsided view of the whole. For a religious order has a hierarchy of authority with a division of labor according to particular individual gifts; has a wide field for strategic planning; and the whole structure is held together by the golden bond of religious obedience.

A Montessori "Third Order"

This would not mean, of course, that there would be any idea of confining the use of Montessori principles to Religious. On the contrary, Montessori herself suggested that there would be a large part to be played by lay people, who would dedicate themselves to the work in a manner similar to that of members of Third Orders in the Dominican, Franciscan and Carmelite movements, and in the same spirit.

Still less would there be any idea of trying to confine the Montessori Movement to Catholics, religious or lay. Just the opposite, in fact, for the whole aim of the Order would be to make known Montessori's ideas on education among "the children of this generation" as well as among "the Children of Light." But the Order itself would act as the incandescent center of a world-wide movement, bringing with it a passionate but disciplined zeal, and acting as a beacon that lights up the way for others.

The Four Spheres of Activity

A Montessori religious order such as Montessori envisaged would have four main spheres of activity:

1) *Education*—the application of Montessori principles to the training of the next generation from the kindergarten,

or "under fives," onward to adolescence. In discussing the matter with Anna Maccheroni, Montessori explained that in the child's first years, those of the "Absorbent Mind," great emphasis would be laid upon what one might call mental hygiene. Just as there are many hospitals and maternity homes run by Religious in which the laws of *physical* hygiene are known and followed, so on this order the laws of *mental* hygiene would equally be studied and as meticulously followed. By this she meant that children should be treated in such a way as to bring out, from the beginning, the characteristic of normality which she discovered. The child would be the center of everything, and everything would be oriented about the physical and mental needs of his development. The application of Montessori principles up to the age of 12 years has already been carried out in a number of schools. Their further application to the age of adolescence has never yet been completely carried out, in the manner Montessori suggested in her *Erde-Kinder* lectures; this, too, could be done eventually by the new Order. (This subject, the Reform of Secondary Education on Montessori lines, is dealt with in a forthcoming book, which is already in preparation.)

2) *Montessori in the Home*—A second "arm" of the Montessori Order would be directed toward the helping of parents in their dealings with their own children in the home. Since Montessori's definition of education is an "aid to life," it is clear that it begins at birth. In fact it begins before birth; and prior to her death Montessori founded a special kind of maternity home in Rome—which still functions. Its aim is to instruct expectant mothers, not only how to take care of their newly-born physically but also mentally, from the moment of their arrival into this most puzzling world.

Incidentally, it is interesting to note that parents are much quicker to appreciate the value of Montessori ideas than are many teachers and professors. This is no doubt because—as was the case with Montessori's first assistants in Rome—parents have not been trained, as teachers have, along the old lines and methods. The parental instinct quickens their whole mental attitude toward infantile psychology and toward anything else which bears on the life of their newly-arrived offspring. There is an immense scope for the dissemination of Montessori's principles in the home, a work which has never been fully written up and properly organized, though already much has, and is being done in this sphere, in connection with many Montessori schools.

The more Montessori principles are practiced in the homes the less "deviated" would the under-five children become before they came to their first class, and the quicker would be their process of "normalization through work" when they did come to school.

3) The Training of Montessori Teachers—The third branch of a Montessori Order would be the setting up, and operating of training colleges for the formation of Montessori directresses. This would be a necessity, for, just as it is true to say, "No Prepared Environment, no Montessori School," so it is equally true to say, "No trained Montessori directress, no Montessori School." This is because there exists in the Montessori system a trinity, which is one and undivided, made up of (I) the children, (II) the Prepared Environment, and (III) the Montessori directress; and if anything goes amiss in the proper functioning of any one of these three something invariably goes wrong with the whole.

As an essential part of this third "arm," the training of teachers, would be the formation of a sort of vigilance committee of experts, which would include all lay people, and non-Catholics also, of long Montessori experience. The aim of this committee would be to guard the name Montessori and the movement that goes under it from the encroachment of other and alien educational ideas and practices which would undermine the fundamental principles on which the Montessori Method is based. This would not mean, of course, that such a committee would act in any way as a brake upon the true and genuine development of Montessori principles and techniques in new and fresh spheres of influence and practice; but it would make sure that these were "true and genuine developments" in the sense that Newman uses the phrase in his famous classic, *An Essay on The Development of Christian Doctrine.*

4) *The Teaching of Religion*—The fourth and the most valuable sphere in which a Montessori religious order would operate, would be the teaching of religion, a work for which by its very nature it would be specially qualified. This would imply the teaching of religion along Montessori principles, which is the theme of this book.

We have shown elsewhere[10] how close is the affinity between the psychology of the Montessori Method and that of the Catholic liturgy—and how apt is the former for giving instruction in the latter—and we indicated at the same time how vast is the field of valuable and rewarding research waiting to be explored. The emphasis which the Ecumenical Council has just placed on the liturgy and the teaching of the liturgy—so that the faithful can take the fullest part in it—is like a finger pointing to the special propriety of founding a Montessori religious order at this moment in the history of the Church.

There have already been a number of indications in the past that the founding of such an Order would be considered with sympathetic attention by those in the highest ecclesiastical positions. Already in 1916 His Holiness Pope Benedict XV,

---

[10] Chapter 8.

who was personally acquainted with Dr. Montessori, had set such a high value on her work that he asked her to draw up a syllabus for use in Catholic schools; but unfortunately he died before this project was carried into execution. We have already noted (in the Foreword) that the late Holy Father, John XXIII—in addressing a Montessori Congress in Venice, when he was Patriarch—said, "It is possible to see a clear analogy between the mission of the Shepherd in the Church and that of the prudent and generous educator in the Montessori Method, who with tenderness, with love, and with a wise evaluation of gifts, knows how to discover and bring to light the most hidden virtues and capacities in the child." (That is, the characteristics of the normalized child.)

It would take far too much space were we to mention all the various connections which Montessori had in her long life with many and various members of the hierarchy in different countries, and the many tributes which they paid to her and her work both during her lifetime and at her death. She was well aware that her work for the Church would have but little permanent value without the support of the authorities; and—like a true daughter of the Church—she was always willing to submit her educational ideas and practices to those whose business it is to evaluate, in the light of Catholic theology and philosophy, all new movements which have a bearing on social and moral life.

Montessori herself, from the very beginning, had the feeling that there was something providential about the manner in which her life, as a university lecturer and practicing physician, was completely and unexpectedly diverted to the sphere of education. In 1917, in a letter to His Excellency Cardinal Pompili, she wrote,

Each of us is called to serve God within the limits that God has ordained,
and in the form He has willed; and my service is the offering of my work.
I believe that this method of education is the instrument God placed in
my hands—for His ends.

The more one considers the Montessori Movement as a
whole, its unpremeditated and astonishing beginning, its
universal appeal and development in so many countries,
its history and development, its beneficial operation in the
natural and supernatural planes, its immense potentialities
for good—not only for individuals but for the Church, and
through the Church for humanity at large—the more the
conviction grows that the founding of such a religious order
to carry on her work would be the fulfillment of her lifelong
desire to serve the Church. It would seal the vow which she
and her first followers took before the Blessed Sacrament in
1910:

Before the majesty of God I desire to consecrate myself to the
service of the Catholic Church, offering myself as a holocaust to
Jesus Christ our Lord. I desire to follow the path of His divine will,
embracing my sweet cross with the intention so truly to live that,
if it be His will, the Church of Christ, in a reformed humanity, may
triumph midst the splendors of civilization.

It is the earnest request of the editor, and his collaborators,
that those who have read this book and appreciated its contents
would join in praying for the intention that almighty God,
in His love and wisdom, would raise up some individual or
group of individuals, who, under the inspiration of the Holy
Spirit, would found such an Order—which would be in fact
(if not in name) *an Order of the Servants of the Children of
Light.*

CHAPTER EIGHT

THE LITURGY AND THE MONTESSORI METHOD

BY E. M. STANDING

At the beginning of this century two important movements originated in the Eternal City which still remains the center of European culture and civilization. One was the *Liturgical Movement* inaugurated by His Holiness Pope Pius X and the other was the *Montessori Movement* started by another great Italian about the same time.

Almost from the beginning, discerning people realized that there existed a certain affinity between these two movements. This became more clear as the years passed. Now—after half a century—this similarity has been commented on in the highest Catholic circles. Thus, in December, 1962, an article was published in the *Osservatore Romano*, the Vatican newspaper, entitled "Il Liturgismo del Metodo Montessori," which might be translated "The Liturgical Nature of the Montessori Method." In this article the writer,[11] after comparing the psychology behind the liturgy with that of the Montessori method, says:

---

[11] Marchesa Sofia Cavalletti

These brief observations should, I believe, be sufficient to justify the expression of the liturgist who spoke of the 'liturgical nature' of the Montessori method, and to explain why such a method is coming to be considered with a particular interest at a time in which a catechetical renewal finds its place in the vast picture of the liturgical renaissance.

This chapter elaborates on this opening theme.

What is the Liturgy?

It is not easy to give a brief and comprehensive reply. By historical derivation the word liturgy meant "the public office voluntarily performed by a wealthy citizen of Greece." Nowadays when people speak of the liturgy they generally refer to the various forms of public worship set down by the Church. Practically all the great religions of the world, both ancient and modern, have some form of liturgy.

The Liturgy is Essential to Our Human Nature

By his very nature, being a compound of spirit and matter, soul and body, man needs something material as well as the purely spiritual. Spirit and matter are not really and essentially in opposition to one another; they are not necessarily conflicting elements that make war upon each other.

The fundamental fact behind Christianity—the Incarnation—means nothing less than this: that God, the Infinite Spirit in the Second Person of the Holy Trinity, "became flesh and dwelt among us" in an indissoluble welding together of spirit and matter. In us, as completed human beings, these two elements are equally essential to our full nature; and will be to all eternity. As man, our Lord Himself rose from the grave in His material body (which He still has), just as our Lady was assumed into heaven in hers. For us, too, a body is necessary for our completion, as necessary as the soul. This is the significance of that article in the Creed, "I believe in the resurrection of the body."

All Religions Have a Liturgy

One sometimes hears the remark that "all the great religions teach more or less the same truths but differ in their outward forms and expressions." As a matter of fact it would be much nearer the mark if one said that "most religions have much the same outward forms—that is an officiating priesthood, an altar and a sacrifice—but they differ in the truths they teach."

It is rather interesting, from this point of view, to speculate on what form of communal worship *could* be carried on by pure spirits. It is of course impossible for us to *imagine* it; and even the author of the Apocalypse is obliged to have recourse to material metaphors, as when he describes the four and twenty elders casting down their golden crowns before the Lamb—just as the prophet Ezekiel describes the coming and going of angels as "living flashes of light"—light, the most immaterial element in the physical universe.

Since writing the above we have come across a passage in a recently published book (*The Liturgy and the Layman* by Rev. James King, S.J.) which so admirably expresses the same idea that we make no apology for quoting it at length:

Communal worship is ... a human necessity. Without active participation of the faithful together, our worship tends to become angelistic, an activity confined to spirit alone.

Such activity neglects man's complete nature. We are not angels; we are intelligent beings composed of soul and body. Our prayer, and most especially our communal, liturgical prayer, must be sufficiently incarnate to answer the needs of our nature. Thus we sing, pray, stand, sit, kneel; we involve our bodies as well as our intellects and will in communal worship. We give our entire selves in worship to God.

We have our example in Christ, who is both man and God. He walked the earth, He ate, slept and preached, and prayed. At the Last Supper He took common foods, bread and wine, blessed them, and gave them to His disciples. 'Take and eat; this is My Body. This is My Blood." Ordinary things like bread, wine, water, oil, He used as signs of supernatural realities: the Body and Blood of Christ, the washing away of sin and imparting of divine life, the healing of soul and body. This is not angelism (p. 6).

People are often very illogical in these matters; and you may find that the very same person, who is shocked by the lighting of a candle to place before the image of a saint, thinks nothing of lighting twenty candles on a birthday cake in honor of a very ordinary person.

Liturgy Outside the Church

Liturgy is something so essential to human beings, when they act together at any solemn function, that it is found outside religion, or anything which is comparably serious. One takes for example the precise and complicated ritual which accompanies the coronation of a king. We get the same sort of thing on a smaller scale in the ordinary etiquette of a court, or such ceremonies as the trooping of the colors, fraternal initiations and so on. Such definite and prescribed ways of doing things seem to spring up spontaneously when people in unison repeatedly perform the same act together.

Some Points About the Liturgy

Let us sum up some of the main characteristics of the liturgy:
1. It is something which arises as a consequence of our twofold nature, e.g., being composed of soul and body.
2. It unites and holds together a group of people engaged in a communal act of worship—even if they are not of the same nation or language. This is especially true of

the great central act of worship—the offering of the Sacrifice of the Mass.

3. It is a means for carrying on the *continuity of worship* and at the same time preserving it from the vagaries and eccentricities of individuals. In times of spiritual slackness, i.e., when religious fervor is at a low ebb, it acts in the Church as a sort of driving-wheel which carries on the momentum of the past into, and through, the present. It also preserves and keeps ever ready for use the forms by which the deepest religious experiences can be expressed.

4. *Actions speak louder than words.* In religion, as in social life, our deepest emotions can often be better expressed by means of actions rather than words. Thus a kiss or a handshake, or even a glance, can speak volumes. And so it is in the religious service. How many such significant actions are incorporated into the liturgy, i.e., kissing the altar, raising the hands, genuflections, raising the eyes to heaven, standing up at the Gospel, the sign of the cross, the lighting of candles, the wonderful service of the Easter Vigil and many other such actions.

5. *The liturgy is charged with symbolic observances.* Symbols are an unrivaled means for bringing certain truths most swiftly and effectively into our minds and hearts: for example, the Crown of Thorns, the mixing of water and wine, the image of the Sacred Heart.

6. Another important function which is carried out by the liturgy is the preserving of a minimum of decency and dignity in religious functions. In this way even a rather careless and indifferent celebrant is kept within certain bounds of decorum during the fulfillment of his office.

7. This also applies to the congregation; making the sign of the cross with holy water on entering the church, genuflecting before entering the pew, standing up when the priest enters—all these and similar actions make for the prevention of slovenliness and careless behavior in the house of God, and give our worship a fitting solemnity, dignity and reverence.

8. Speaking historically, the liturgy has been the means of incorporating into regular public worship the inspirations of holy men in the past. Thus, somebody must have been the first who, in the depths of his emotion, stooped down and kissed the altar on which our Mass was celebrated, or where the bones of the martyrs were enshrined. In the same way, someone must have been the first to kiss the book of the Gospel after he had finished reading from it, just as it was probably some far off presbyter or deacon who urged the people to stand at the reading of the Gospel. These actions were felt to be so apposite that they were incorporated, one by one, into the regular performance of the rite. And thus, century after century, the liturgy grew and developed like a great work of art under the inspiration of the Holy Spirit.

9. We must not of course forget that some of the actions of the liturgy are more than symbolic. The sacraments are in fact the actual channels of grace, for Christ Himself acts when the rite is performed. There, too, in the most striking form we realize how wonderfully our Lord, in His dealing with us, adopted means most suitable to our twofold nature of spirit and matter. "He knoweth our frame; He remembereth that we are dust."

10. The liturgy is something which makes its appeal to the learned and unlearned alike—to those who cannot read, as well as to the scholar; and further, it is an appeal which is independent of language, and so can be understood and appreciated by all.

Children and the Liturgy

By their very nature children are inveterate liturgists. At the early age of two-and-a-half to four they are most insistent on having things done in the correct, that is the accustomed, way. In fact, I have heard Montessori compare the small child at this *Sensitive Period to Order* to a master of ceremonies at a religious function. And, as we have pointed out in other parts of this book, it is possible for small children to appreciate much of the liturgy *at a sensorial level* even before the age of reason.

A Profound Affinity

A natural affinity exists between the Montessori Method and the liturgy which is due to a common psychology. That is why it is easy to teach the liturgy to small children by the Montessori Method. It will help us to understand the nature of this deep underlying affinity if we consider Montessori's doctrine of:

The Periphery and the Center

We can regard the child, says Montessori, from two different aspects. First, we have the "periphery" of his personality; by this she means that part of his personality which is revealed to us when we note the external aspects of his being. We see him using his sense organs—sight, hearing and touch, and so on. We observe his actions, his different movements, large and small. It is at the periphery that we see him choosing this thing and not that. In short, we are concerned with the external aspect of his personality, that part which we see in contact with the outside world. And this is the part of his personality which is immediately accessible to us.

Then we have, secondly, the "Center." This is that more mysterious part of his personality which belongs exclusively to himself. Here the child's creative intelligence is at work; here his will operates; in this invisible center, inaccessible to us, things take their origin; it is here that choices and decisions are made. It is, in short, the innermost citadel of his personality. The Center is not merely a sort of mechanism which reflects, records and responds to stimuli from the outside world. It can better be compared to a glowing forge where the intellect, together with the emotions and the will—working in unison—create the man-that-is-to-be.

As to how exactly this is done, says Montessori, we need not worry ourselves. It is the child's secret. For the Montessori directress it is enough to know that this mysterious Center *is* at work, without her being too anxious as to *how* it works. The most creative processes of nature usually take place in secrecy; and nature has many psychological secrets which we do not understand; into which, for practical purposes, it is not necessary for us to pry.

The Interaction between the Center and the Periphery

Between these two elements or poles of his personality there is a constant interaction. "We are convinced," says Montessori, "through long experience that the child's personality grows by a welding together of these two elements of his personality, thereby constructing his own mind, and expressing himself at the same time. While the child is working actively, at the periphery with material things, at one and the same time he gathers in sensory experience, builds himself up, and expresses himself. For him self-creation is the highest form of self-expression.

"This interaction between the visible periphery and the invisible center goes on unceasingly. It is like the rhythm of a wave that never ceases, the beating of a heart that never stops."

A Contrast in Methods

In most pedagogical methods, the teacher usually addresses himself directly to the Center. Her job is to get the idea she wishes the child to absorb *directly* across to his intelligence. She is not concerned with his "periphery" except to see that he is paying attention to *her* and not to his neighbors, or not fiddling with something under the desk. This approach is exemplified by the old Herbartian "Steps," according to which the teacher has prepared her lesson in advance . . . Preparation, Presentation, Development, Application, etc. Like a preacher in the pulpit, or a lecturer at a university, she applies herself *directly* to the child's intelligence; and to his will, also, for he is *obliged* to attend.

In the Montessori approach it is quite different. Except at certain times the Montessori directress does not concern herself directly with the "center." Her job is "to feed the periphery" which she does by means of specially devised teaching materials. Each of these is so constructed as to set up an activity to the periphery, a manipulation of materials— which often involves movement of the whole body—as, for instance, in the number rods or the time-line. The directress shows the child exactly how to use the particular material in question. It might be the movable alphabet, or a material for teaching the Parts of Speech, or for Long Division. And when she sees the child has "cottoned on" to the manner of using it properly she goes away and leaves him to it. She knows that, as long as he uses the material correctly, his repeated activity with it will set going, and keep going, a corresponding activity deep down in the Center.

That is why if you go into a Montessori school the chances are that, at any moment, the majority of the children are working individually at various materials quite independently of the directress. The activity which you will then see is a peripheral one; but along with this the children are learning from the material itself. In fact, it is true auto-education which is going on. For the particular item of knowledge, which is as it were latent in each material, gradually impresses itself on the child's mind as he works away happily with it at the periphery.

The Point of Contact

Each of these material occupations acts as a "Point of Contact" between the Center and an external reality. It is through this Point of Contact, and the repeated activity which it brings about, that this external reality makes itself known to the child's intelligence. Take that young fellow you see over there in the corner, working away at the multiplication table-board. Without going into detail we may say that this material permits him to work out for himself—by means of pegs and a special number peg-board—the multiple of any number up to ten he chooses. Actually, at the moment he is at work on the seven times table, and has got as far as six sevens equal forty-two. He has just counted the six sevens on the peg-board and, having done so, records the number on a prepared slip of paper. He proceeds now to make the next multiple of seven, and having done so counts it, then records it; and so on until he comes to ten sevens and the table is completed.

It is in fact a genuine mathematical research; and at the end of it he is not the same as he was at the beginning. A genuine portion of the great world of mathematical reality outside himself has recorded itself at his Center. A reality from *without* has—passing through the Point of Contact—made itself known *within* him, and has become a part of himself.

This is a very different process from letting the child just play with the pegs in any manner his fancy might take him— as, for instance, to "make a garden" or "a pretty pattern." For in such occupations there takes place only an outward movement from within. Nothing from without has been recorded; no new reality has presented itself; no new piece of knowledge has entered the mind from without. As far as new knowledge is concerned, the child is left exactly where he was. Not that there is anything wrong in letting the child do this; but only that we wish to point out that—in the case of a child thus working at his own whim with the material—he is master of the whole situation in the sense that he dominates the material, making it subservient to *his* will. That is to say he is not subject to the discipline of an external reality.

You may say, "But this is a form of self-expression." And so it is up to a point, and not without its value as such; but it is emphatically *not* a process by which the child's intelligence grows and expands by its own self-activity; as it absorbs and digests new facts from without.

The Point of Contact Brings Limitation

There is another important feature of this Point of Contact which is formed by the Montessori materials, and it is this: that the *Point of Contact always brings with it a definite limitation and precision,* that exactitude which comes inevitably with order. This is because the directress always insists on the child using the materials in a definite and precise manner. For it is only by so doing that the materials will yield their secret, that is the portion of knowledge which is concealed within each of them. It is this item of real knowledge which impresses itself on the child's intelligence *pari passu* with the manipulative activity which we see taking place at the periphery.

Many persons criticize the Montessori Method on this account, inferring that—by this limitation and precision, this prescribed manner of working with the materials—we are inhibiting the child's free development. But the contrary is true. It is just by carrying out this prescribed limitation, involved in the right use of the materials, that the child's further development is assured. Thus, you will find that it is the very child who has been working with the geometric insets *in the orthodox manner*—that is feeling their contours with his first two fingers, or putting them out on the corresponding cards, or learning their names, rather than doing anything he likes with them—who will joyfully discover that the whole environment about him is full of geometric forms which he had never noticed before. It is this child who will excitedly announce that his plate is a circle, or that the window is a rectangle, or that the piece of paper he has just cut off from the corner of his drawing paper is a triangle.

This is not dissimilar to that form of limitation which precedes progress in the spiritual life. "Straight is the way and narrow is the gate," says the Gospel, "that leads to salvation." The gate indeed is narrow—yes—but not the wide world of spiritual realities to which it leads. These remarks apply equally to religious materials.

Keys to the Universe

As we have said elsewhere: [12]

Each of the Montessori materials, when properly used, opens up new vistas of experience, reveals new wonders in the world around him, wonders which have always been present but have hitherto remained unnoticed. That is why Montessori calls them "Keys to the Universe."

"Some persons," says Montessori, "complain that we give too few things to the children. That is because they do not realize that what we do is to give them the means to see and understand better. They confuse the keys to the universe with the universe itself.

"Let us keep, then, constantly before us this picture of the child mind, called through the point of contact to a small work, limited and exact—to a real work not a make-believe. Just as a piece of music played in the children's presence summons them from making any kind of movements to the performance of precise and limited movements in accordance with the rhythm of the music; so, in the mental sphere, the point of contact summons the mind of the child from wandering at large in fantasy to something definite and real, which opens up a new pathway."

The Center and the Periphery; The Point of Contact and the Liturgy

It only remains for us to underline the points of similarity which arise in the mind when one applies the Montessori doctrine of the "Center and the Periphery" and the "Point of Contact" to the Catholic liturgy.

In those parts of the Mass which are read aloud in the vernacular, or when the priest is giving a homily, the appeal is directly to our intelligences, to the "Center."

But there are many times during the celebration of the Mass, and other liturgical functions, when what is going on makes its appeal to us in a more indirect manner. All through

---

[12] *Maria Montessori—Her Life and Work,* pp. 220-221.

the Liturgy of the Word and the Liturgy of the Eucharist, we find a great variety of symbolical actions—signs of the cross, beating of the breast, genuflections, special postures for the hands, washing of the hands, raising of the eyes, bowing the head and kissing the altar or the missal. Some of these actions are for the priest only to perform. But in many of them the faithful are also invited to participate, such as the sign of the cross at the beginning of Mass, or three times on the forehead, lips and breast, before the reading of the Gospel; or striking the breast at the *Confiteor* and the "Lord, I am not worthy."

In the sacraments, as we all know, there are material elements and strictly prescribed actions. Take baptism, for example, with its carefully ordained ritual and its use of such elements as water, salt and oil. In holy orders the hands of the ordained are bound together by the bishop at the rite of ordination.

All these external actions—these signs, symbols, postures, movements—make their appeal to our souls *indirectly* at the "periphery" of our personality. They are in fact "points of contact" between them and the great world of spiritual realities outside us.

As the Christian year revolves, holy Church in her divine wisdom places before us a whole series of such "sensible signs" often to be accompanied by our own actions. For the Church, like the Montessori Method, realizes that for children "visual aids" are not enough; they need "sensory-motor aids." And are we not all children in the eyes of the Church—her "Children of Light"—and, as such, in need of actions as well as visible aids?

How deeply are our hearts touched at Christmastime, as we kneel before the crib, and ponder the ineffable wonder of the Lord of the universe lying helpless and utterly dependent in the manger! As we meditate over the mystery of the Mother who gave birth to God and God who created His Mother, are not our souls stirred with thoughts beyond the reach of our minds? Again, how significant is the tableau of the Epiphany where we behold the Three Kings, wise with all the ancient lore of the East, bowing down in simple adoration before the Infant who is God and Man—dispelling at once and forever by His divine radiance the "Maya" or "Illusion," the contempt for matter, that lies at the heart of so many Oriental philosophies.

And as we come to the beginning of Lent what sermon on the frailty of our tenure of this mortal existence could be more effective than the ceremony in which the priests make the sign of the cross, in ashes, on the foreheads of those who must all return to dust when the appointed moment comes?

But most of all it is in the celebrations of the great mysteries of the Eastertide that the Church excels herself in the magnificent ceremonies that have been built up around the passion, death and resurrection of her divine Founder. In her age-long wisdom and ingenuity, she has thought of many things which would never have occurred to us, a multitude of wonderful symbols and dramatic actions. Who has not, for instance, experienced a sort of mild shock on coming into church on Passion Sunday to find all the statues covered up, to be kept out of sight until the great rejoicing on Easter morning? We had forgotten—but the Church never forgets.

There is something irresistible about the progress of the liturgy. It moves forward with the inevitability of a glacier; but at the heart of it there is nothing cold, like ice, but rather the burning passion of divine Love. And when we come to the Second Passion Sunday (Palm Sunday), the Church, instead of contenting herself with reading the account of the triumphal entry into Jerusalem, places before us the Blessing of the Palms, then the procession, to be followed later by the distribution of the palms to the faithful, who take them home to put them in a conspicuous place on their walls. In this way the memory of the great event lingers on like a fragrant perfume for many weeks.

And so on through all the rest of Holy Week. What wonderful and dramatic representations and actions does not the Church place before us: the stripping of the altars on Maundy Thursday, the empty tabernacle, the altar of repose, the Good Friday liturgy with its veneration of the holy cross. Then in cathedral churches, we have the wonderfully tense and dramatic ceremony of *Tenebrae.* As the lights go out, one by one, we almost feel that we are being abandoned to the powers of darkness—always so ready to drag us down to the pit. But the One Light remains, and, though it is hidden from us for a moment, it reveals itself as unquenchable; for, although "this is your hour and the Power of Darkness . . . The Prince of this World has nothing in Me. . . . Take courage for I have conquered the world." The newly appointed Vigil of Easter service is rich in all manner of moving ceremonies— the Lighting of the Paschal Candle, with the fixing of the five grains of incense in the form of a cross, the beautiful prayer *"Lumen Christi"* repeated three times; and the lighting of all the candles in the church from the original light. How beautiful and how admirable are all these, and how deeply they touch our souls. There comes the great moment of the *"Exsultet."* Finally at the *Gloria* the organ plays again after its long silence, the bells peal out, the statues are uncovered, and voices are raised in praise and thanksgiving. Indeed it seems as though the whole universe exults in the victory of Life over death.

> *"Mors et vita duello conflixere mirando:*
> *Dux vitae mortuus, regnat vivus"*

(Together death and life in a strange conflict strove.
The Prince of Life who died now lives and reigns.)

A Children's Liturgy

We might mention that Montessori had the intention of working out a special sort of Holy Week Liturgy adapted for small children, not of course in any way as a substitute for the ceremonies of the Church, but something in addition and particularly suitable to be carried out by the children themselves in the Atrium. The specially constructed "Liturgical Table" and the little scenes enacted around it give us some idea as to the way Montessori would have carried out this work; as do the various other means she devised to help children, described in her Barcelona experiment, and in her talks on the Atrium.

Though Montessori was never able to carry out to the full her ideas in this sphere, she nevertheless laid down the general lines on which it should be done; and since her death in 1952 a number of her followers have been working along these lines, particularly in connection with certain Montessori schools in Italy and France. In fact, one might say that a sort of children's liturgy is coming into existence, the aim of which is to make use of the small child's interest in sensory-motor activities in the pre-six years.

Unquestionably we have here a wide and fruitful field for further research; and, as new developments come to be worked out and tested, they will no doubt in due time be collected and collated and—subject to ecclesiastical approval—written up and published.

The Point of Contact in the Liturgy

The parallel between the psychology of the liturgy and that

of the Montessori Method needs to be mentioned. We noted above that the Point of Contact in the Montessori Method always brings with it a certain limitation, the limitation of precision, and in this context we commented on the fact that the Montessori directress insists on the children using the teaching materials in a definite and prescribed way.

So it is in the liturgy. The "points of contact" which the Church prepares in the liturgy, in order to bring our souls in touch with the great truths of the spiritual life, are nothing if not definite and precise.

She leaves nothing to chance or to the vagaries of the individual. Montessori herself once said—in discussing the liturgy: "The Church is a society which has fixed certain movements and words; and this very precision is not caprice: it is something which corresponds to the spiritual life." In concluding this comparison between the psychological method of the liturgy and that of the Montessori Method we cannot do better than to end it with further extracts from the article from the *Osservatore Romano* quoted in the opening paragraphs.

If the concrete nature of the Bible and the liturgy—shown in stories and in "sensible signs"—are a necessity in pastoral work in general and correspond to the particular exigencies of our time, how much more necessary are they when they are dealing with the catechism for children who, more than adults, feel the need of the support of a sure foundation in the concrete in order that they may take off for their flight into the realm of supersensible reality!

It is for this reason that among the various experiments that have been carried out in recent years we would like to draw attention to the opportune nature of those experiments in teaching the catechism which have been conducted according to the principles of Montessori; because we would venture to say that the Montessori Method presents striking affinities with what one might call 'Method of the liturgy,' that is to say, with the pedagogical method of the Catholic Church itself. In fact, I believe that one can truly say that the great value in the Montessori Method lies precisely in this— that it has rediscovered and put into practice in a wide field that pedagogical method which the Church in her millennial wisdom has always used.

Let us admit straightaway that the liturgy and the Montessori Method operate on two different planes—the one working toward conferring upon human beings the gift of eternal life; the other working toward a psychic development which is balanced and complete. The one (the latter) can fulfill only an ancillary function in comparison with the former, which aims at preparing children who are psychologically healthy, and therefore furnished with those requisites which render them more receptive to the gift of divine grace.

The Prepared Environment

(a) In the Church:

This being granted let us note that the Church has always taken the greatest care in the preparation of her places of worship. Such care is due without doubt to a respect for the holy place and for the Divine Presence within it. But this does not exhaust the reasons for that care which the Church manifests in the preparation of its places of worship. It is also the desire of the Church that the place of worship should offer an assistance to the faithful in their religious life. With this aim in view she seeks to create a special atmosphere by means of architecture, the play of lights and shadows, and music. With this aim in view, too, the inside walls of the church are adorned with images intended to arouse and sustain religious ideas and sentiments. It is enough for us to call to mind the great medieval basilicas which were called the 'Bible of the Poor' or the 'Illustrated Catechism.' And if we go still further back in time we see that places of assembly, only occasionally used, like the catacombs, were prepared with the same care, in order to place before the eyes of the persecuted Christians images apt to arouse in them sentiments of faith and hope. There were found most frequently pictures of the Good Shepherd "who saves His sheep from the cunning of the wolves." And there we find representations of Jonah rescued from the depths of the sea, or the three young men walking unharmed in the midst of the flames, or of Daniel unhurt in the lions' den ... all pictures which speak of the mortal dangers from which God saves His faithful. There, too, we find the raising of Lazarus telling us that beyond physical death is the hope in the Resurrection.

(b) In the Montessori Method:

One of the basic principles of the Montessori Method is the preparation of a stimulating environment in which children are to live. Anyone who knows this Method has seen, at least in photographs, those rooms supplied with furniture of dimensions suitable to the proportions of the children. The aim of all this is to create around the child conditions which make it possible for them to carry out certain determined actions. If the child, who needs to be able to move about and to be active, finds himself always confronted with furniture and objects which, because they are too large or too heavy, limit, or actually downright prevent his activity, we would see him little by little constrained to give up these activities. Then those energies—which should be used to construct his personality—would end by being extinguished, or by being deviated from their channels. This then is the provident function of the prepared environment with which the Montessori Method aims at assisting the physical and mental life of the children precisely as the Church considers her 'prepared environment' as an aid to religious life.

Man a Unity of Mind and Body

One definition of the liturgy runs as follows: 'It is an assemblage of the sensible signs of the sanctification and worship of the Church.' Let us pause a moment to consider the significance of the phrase 'sensible signs.' They stand for something which strikes the senses; something in which there is incarnated a supernatural reality. Human beings cannot perceive directly a supernatural reality unless it takes form in a sensible element. And this is what liturgists call the 'law of incarnation.' The Church knows that man is not a pure spirit, and therefore a discarnate form of worship would not correspond to his most vital needs. In the whole course of the Scriptures the Church considers man—as he is—as a unity in which you cannot separate a body and a spirit, so much so that a body separated from the spirit is a corpse.

Another essential point in the Montesson Method is the use of a sensorial material for the little ones, and of cultural materials for the older ones. In both we are dealing with objects which are offered to the children in order that by manipulating—arranging and re-arranging them— they come either to the perfecting of their senses or to the acquisition of a cultural nature. In this latter case the use of the materials is of such a nature that this learning takes place, not only by means of the intellectual faculty, but also by bringing into play all his faculties—sight, hearing, touch, and movement. And it happens in this way precisely because the child is not only an intellect, but a creature who should be taken into consideration as a unity of mind and body.

The Church the True End of the Montessori Method

The first application of the Montessori Method to the teaching of religion takes us back to the beginning of the century as it was carried out by Maria Montessori herself. She has left several books on this subject and a certain amount of material—some of which is still unpublished. In the course of time this experiment was taken up again in various Montessori schools, particularly in England and in Ireland. Perhaps the most complete application of Montessori principles in this field at the present moment, is the Montessori Center in Rennes, France, where the whole life of the school is polarized around the liturgy. More recently—although it has been going on for practically a decade—the same work has been carried on in Rome at the Maria Montessori School for Religion.[13]

All these experiments have demonstrated not only the efficacy of the Montessori Method in religious formation, *but that the Method itself finds its completion only in the religious preparation of children.* Montessori was already aware of this at the time of her Barcelona experiment in Spain. Many things which the children do in her schools, she said, remain deprived of their full significance until they find their full *raison d'être* in the Church.

Grace Builds on Nature

It is without a doubt true that the Montessori Method prepares in the children a harmonious mental development

---

[13] From "*Il Liturgismo de Metodo Montessori*" by Marchesa Sofia Cavalletti, *Osservatore Romano,* Dec. 29, 1962.

(psyche sana); but a harmonious mental development is not the end in itself because in man there is a capacity for a "third dimension" that of the supernatural which completed the other dimensions bringing them to their true end. We can express it thus: the Montessori Method is an aid to the development of the human spirit; but the human spirit cannot find its complete expansion anywhere else but in God.

CHAPTER NINE

CATECHISM FOR THE YOUNG

BY THE REVEREND MOTHER ISABEL EUGENIE, R.A.

Montessori says that the child during its early infancy— indeed while still a baby in arms—absorbs impressions from the environment. It reminds one of the way blotting paper absorbs ink, or a sensitive film the impressions of light. If there is religion in the environment he absorbs that also. Dr. Montessori told us how, at Naples, she used to observe the peasant women who came to the church carrying their babies in their arms, and she watched them praying. The child was there, quite quiet and without understanding, but he felt the atmosphere of silence and of prayer. During the ceremonies the baby heard religious music, while the beauty of the paintings, of the colors, of the gold on the decorations, entered into him. Montessori said that everything that penetrates into the soul of the child at this early age makes a profound impression on him. She often thought that when children were deprived, while quite tiny, of this atmosphere, of this family life through which they learned religion by breathing it in, as it were, their faith might be less vivid and less deep later on. This makes us realize the importance of family prayers, of holy pictures and crucifixes on the walls of the home, of holy water, and of sacramentals generally.

A priest who lived in the mountains of Wales, in a place where there are few Catholics, and most of these not very practical, once told a meeting of teachers that he had reconciled to God numbers of these souls on their deathbed, all brought back to the Church by the impressions and the knowledge given to them in their first seven years.

The small child is altogether innocent and lacking in experience. He has a deep sense of wonder. The most ordinary thing to us, is to him extraordinary. He has a real sense of the supernatural, a real intuition. Everything in his soul carries him to God. It is at this age that he receives his first ideas about God—a terrific responsibility for parents. The child will make his own idea of God according to the way that God has been presented to him. On this idea of God, which we have given to him, depends his whole future spiritual life, his relations with God for the whole of the rest of his life, and perhaps his eternity. It is necessary to have people of deep faith and true piety to give the children their first idea of God. Whoever does this must be deeply sincere.

"God Loves Me!"

A little child easily becomes interested in God, if he is convinced that God is interested in him. Children respond to personal love of them. The eternal love of God, His choice of the child's soul from all eternity, and His creation of it individually, delights even quite tiny children; and they become instantly interested in their Creator.

It fascinates them to hear the "God loves me" story which names them. "Long, long ago, when there was nothing—nothing at all and no people at all—when no one was there to think of you (John/ Mary) or to love or to want you except the great God—that in that long ago, God, there all by Himself, was thinking of you, was loving you, was wanting you. God knew that some day He would make you, because He loved and chose you, out of all others that He might have made.

"Then, at last, God *did* make you. He gave you a body and a soul. He gave you an angel to look after you. He gave you a father and a mother to take care of you . . . And into the heart of Father and Mother He put a tiny spark of His own great love for you. That is why Father and Mother love you so much—more than anyone else in the whole world does."

This lesson has to be repeated many times, as indeed each lesson has to be, for small children love the same thing over and over again.

They love to hear *their own name spoken,* and wait with breathless attention until their turn comes. A class of over twenty children under six will wait, silent and expectant, for the teacher to say each of their names. Once one of the children, hidden in the background, was not named by the directress. The child was quite upset. She came out of her place. "But what about me?" she said tearfully, "doesn't He love me too?"

A little girl of four, living in Sweden, had this lesson read to her by her mother. The child was quite indifferent until she heard her own name, and then at once she became interested. She made her mother repeat the lesson, and subsequently used to ask for it, and would listen with evident contentment.

"God Gave Me Another Life"

Our representative child, John/Mary, is next delighted to learn that "not only did God choose out of love to make you, but He loved you so much that *He was ready to give you another life besides your own;* a share in His own great life.

So that you have really got two lives: your own little life, that you got on the day you were born when God sent you with your angel to your father and mother; and God's life, which you got on your greater birthday; the greatest and most important day of your life; the day of your baptism."

The children love a description of that day; of the baby's preparation (christening dress, godparents, etc.) and their own unconsciousness of everything. "The most important day of Mary's life, and yet she knew nothing at all about it, and did not care at all," is a phrase that invariably makes them burst out with some remark "but God knew, and our Lady and the angels"; or, "I wish I *had* known," or "I am glad I know *now*."

Children love to hear over and over again in detail all that happened in their soul that day, unseen by anybody but God: Adam's sin washed away; God's life poured in; and God—the Blessed Trinity—coming into them to make their soul His home.

Often when asked where God lives, the tiniest children say, "Inside me," or "In my heart," and pat themselves with a smile of satisfaction.

A little child of three and a half, on hearing this lesson repeated many times, far from growing tired of it, would hug herself with delight when it began again, and rock herself backward and forward, pattering her little feet on the floor, and murmuring to herself, "I love that day, I love that day."

A restless child of five was told one day by her governess that she was so naughty she must have the devil inside her. "I can't have the devil inside me," she answered indignantly, "because I've been baptized and God is inside me. He won't go unless I do a big sin, and I'm too small to do one."

Children are delighted when they realize how much God has given them out of His love. They now know that they have a family in heaven as well as their own on earth. God is their Father, our Lady is their mother, the saints their brothers and sisters in Christ and the angels their friends.

"God Wanted Me to See Him"

"But it was not enough for God to create Mary out of nothing, and then give her another life in baptism. He wanted to do more than that. He loved Mary so much that He wanted her to know exactly what He was like, so that Mary could love Him back. But God's home is in heaven and Mary has never been to heaven; and so she has not seen God. So God came down from heaven to earth and became like Mary herself, a child. He became even smaller than Mary is now: He became a tiny babe." So now comes the story of Bethlehem, and the other Joyful Mysteries. "Little Jesus is God. He became a child like you." It is God *à leur taille*, to their own size, if one can so express it.

"God Needed a Mother"

A very small child—the newly-born—knows only himself and his mother. The mother is everything to him—his world, his universe. She is for him security, love, joy, warmth, nourishment, refuge, and rest. When God became a Child He needed a mother just as other children do. God made His Mother, and He made her the holiest, the loveliest of all— holier even than the angels. And she is our mother, too—our mother in heaven. So we have two mothers, one on earth and one in heaven.

Children like to see large pictures on these subjects hung on the walls of their classroom or Atrium. They will stand before them in silence, gazing at them for a long time. They are thinking; they are loving; they are contemplating.

"God Wants to Meet Me"

When children know these stories very well—and they love to hear them over and over again—another new wonder is added. When God became a little baby and grew up into a man—all this happened a long time ago—a hundred years ago—long before Mary was made. But this was not yet enough for God's great love. He loved Mary herself and He did not want to be just a history story for her, but He wants to meet Mary herself; and He longs for Mary to meet Him.

"So He made Himself even tinier than a little baby. He made Himself look like a small, round, white piece of bread. And Jesus looking like bread has a special name: He is called the Blessed Sacrament. He lives in the church which is His house. He is living on the altar, in the tabernacle. There you can go and visit Him, and speak to Him whenever you like. He longs for the day when He can come into your heart, and make you His little church. That will be the glorious day of your first Communion."

A Warning to the Teacher: Love, not Fear

Great care should be taken *never to frighten* little children. We must never tell them anything that is not true, such as: "If you are naughty, God won't love you any more." When telling about the Passion, too vivid a picture of the physical sufferings of our Lord should be avoided. Children can be greatly disturbed at these. An ordinary crucifix is sufficient when explaining to the children about our Lord's death on the cross.

Again care must be taken in telling them the story of the Fall. God must not be presented as angry or revengeful in punishing Adam and Eve. It must be explained to them clearly that when Adam and Eve disobeyed God, they lost the great gift of sanctifying grace, and in this way separated themselves from God. They could not get back this great gift by themselves, that is why Jesus came.

Children's Interest in Words

Children between the ages of four and nine are intensely interested in words. They love new and difficult words, and they are very proud of knowing how to employ them. (Montessori once remarked in a lecture that a child of five is much more pleased to have an uncle with a name like "Nebuchadnezzar," than "Tom," something worthwhile wrapping your tongue around!) They love the long and difficult words in which the dogmas are expressed, and enjoy learning the word for word of the catechism, *once the meaning is clear in their minds*.

For example, small children learn about God's life in the soul, and later on they call it "grace"; then "sanctifying grace" and then the "supernatural life."

They are most interested in their natural and supernatural lives, and their natural and supernatural gifts. A child of seven remarked one day: "There is Someone—God—who can't have anything supernatural—because it's all natural to Him."

A child of five, on hearing that God's life in the soul is called grace, exclaimed delightedly: " 'Hail, Mary, full of grace'—that means she was full of God's life then." And a four-year-old added, "Do you think if I asked our Lady she would give some of her full of grace to Daddy and Mummy?"

This teaching of doctrine makes their piety solid and real with nothing sentimental or sticky about it. Indeed the children are apt to show amusement at some of the prayers and pictures brought out as suitable for tiny children.

One day a group of children between five and eight years were looking at a picture book in which the angels were shown as babies with wings. They unanimously declared that the pictures were sweet, but several said: "Angels aren't really like that, are they?"

And one asked, "Did the person who drew these pictures know there aren't any baby angels?"

"But why do they always paint angels with wings?" broke in another.

"Well," said a seven-year old, "What can they do? Angels are think and love, and we can't draw think and love, so they must do something."

The Small Child and the Truths of Doctrine

Our first lessons therefore should be to make God real and personal to the child. On this foundation a solid edifice of doctrine can be built.

Little children respond not only to love, but also to truth. They like simple and elementary things, and simple and elementary truths. They like dogma, and they can assimilate and appreciate a surprising amount of solid doctrine. They like the Athanasian Creed, for example, the first part of which, about the Blessed Trinity, is most helpful for teaching doctrine to children under six years of age; while the second part, on the Incarnation, is invaluable for teaching those of seven and eight. It is astonishing how much they turn these things over in their minds and how deeply they go into them. The questions they ask, and the remarks they make, are proof enough of this. Sometimes, after a few lessons on sin, grace, or the sacraments, the whole lesson or more is passed in simply answering their questions. Indeed, often the children answer each other themselves, and the teacher has only to approve or to correct what they say.

Ex Ore Infantium

After a lesson on sin, a seven-year old remarks: "Well, really then there is only one sin in the world, and that is disobedience."

"Why is it we can only be baptized once?" a new student asked. "Because once we are children of God we are that for good and all," answered another.

"Besides, once Adam's sin is washed off, it can't be washed off again," said a boy of seven, "because it can't come on again."

"You see," said a third, "it's like being born, that can't keep on happening; once you're here, you're here."

"How old is God?" asked a five-year old.

Another of the same age, "Terribly old. He's older than anyone else."

"Yes, but He's really quite young," said a child of six, "because He's always the same."

"You are silly," from another six, "He hasn't any age at all. He never began."

"He did have a birthday, though," said another five, "because His birthday is Christmas Day."

"Yes," said a seven from a distance (she did not belong to that catechism group), "I know how old He was last Christmas —1965—but that's as a man. He isn't any age as God—but they're too small to understand that, aren't they, Mother?"

"Did Adam and Eve have guardian angels before the Fall, or only after?" was another question.

The Liturgical Year

Then again, there is the following of the liturgical cycle. During the school year it is easy to give each term its own marked liturgical aspect. The pictures on the walls can be those of the season; also the prayers said in the daily visit to the Blessed Sacrament. During Advent the children like to sing *Veni, Domine, et noli tardere;* and often say it during the day at the end of various prayers.

At the singing lesson, hymns can be learned which contain the devotion and dogma proper to the season in words suitable to children. They like these so much that they will often sing them spontaneously during drawing and handwork. One day a five-year old, on hearing that our Lord went up to heaven forty days after Easter, exclaimed: "Oh, there was another forty days in our Lord's life too," and she quoted:

> "Forty days did Jesus stay
> All alone to fast and pray."

Another thing that children like is to have special feast altars decorated with texts from the Office of the day. They look forward to having these altars, and learn the texts by heart, and include them in their prayers. They greatly appreciate the words of the Gospel, and much admire homemade picture books with extracts from the Gospels copied into them. Many verses from the Old Testament appeal to them also.

The Mass

Most of all, children love to hear lessons on the Mass. They are interested not only in the ceremonies which they can easily learn with a model altar and miniature vestments and altar vessels, but also in the Missal itself and the Montessori Mass cards.

One of our children once taught her own mother how to follow the Mass in her Missal, much to the mother's great astonishment. Children of about eight years will eagerly follow the actual words of the Mass, once they understand in a general way what the prayers and ceremonies mean.

"I do love following what the priest says," said another child of eight coming out of Mass, "but it's sometimes awfully hard to keep up."

"But you can't understand all those long prayers," said the directress.

"No, but that doesn't matter, somehow. It's nice all the same. And in any case, God does."

First Communion

Frequentation of the sacraments is the very best way of interesting very little children in religion. By *very little children,* I mean children under seven. It is at this early age, 5-6, that the child is easily prepared for his first Communion. It is generally thought that the age for first Communion is the age at which a child can distinguish between good and evil and make his first confession. But that is not what St. Pius X asked for in his Decree *Quam Singulari* on the first Communion of little children. This decree met with much resistance, and many years later Pope Pius XI asked Cardinal Jorio, Prefect of the Congregation of the Sacraments, to write a commentary on *Quam Singulari* explaining precisely what was meant about the first Communion age. The obligation for Communion is different from the obligation for confession. Children may go to Communion when they can distinguish between the Blessed Sacrament and ordinary bread, and when they have some knowledge, suited to the capacity of their age, of the truths necessary to salvation. The obligation for confession holds only when a person is in mortal sin. A child may go to Communion before making his first confession, says Cardinal Jorio, with the consent of his spiritual Father—"in the white robe of his baptismal innocence."

St. Pius X had practiced what he preached in this respect—witness the following incident: receiving in audience one day a father and mother and a little child of four, St. Pius asked if the child had made her first Communion.

The pope asked the child to make the sign of the cross. She did so.

"Whom do you receive when you go to Communion?" he asked.

"Jesus," was the answer.

"Come to my Mass tomorrow morning, and I will give you Holy Communion myself."

At a first Communion of children of six and seven years of age, there was also a little girl of four and a half. There were many who criticized this and disapproved of it. The child went to the altar rail with the others and received the sacred Host. But when the others went back to their places, she remained where she was, on her knees. The directress whispered to her to return to her place. She did not move, however, but turned her face and the directress saw that a rim of the Host, which was too big for her tiny mouth, was showing on her lips. The child evidently knew that she must not touch the Blessed Sacrament with her fingers. The directress drew the priest's attention to it and he took the rim of the Host and put it into her mouth and the child returned calmly and quietly to her place. Many people were struck by this. The child obviously understood whom she was receiving.

If anyone is astonished at the idea that children may go to Communion before their first confession, they should remember that little children have no malice. What separates the soul from God is deliberate sin, and little children are completely incapable of it.

During this initial stage—as we have pointed out above—children should learn how much God loves them, and all that He has done for them to prove His love, and that He asks for their love in return. Given the opportunity they go often to Holy Communion, as St. Pius X wished, in order that our Lord should take possession of them more and more, before they are capable of sin. They should be taught everything that gives them joy and security surrounding them from morning to night with the love of God. They should learn to think of Him and to speak to Him spontaneously. They should be filled with the desire of heaven, their home, for the possession of which God created them. Should they be poor, suffering, deprived in any way, they will taste more than the others of the fullness of Eternal Joy.

The Juniors—Ages 7-12 Years

The second period, from seven to twelve years old, has different characteristics. At this age, children are very interested in questions of right and wrong; their moral sense is developing. Great care must be taken so that they do not lose their assurance and their security in God's love for them personally, when they begin to learn about sin, the Commandments and conscience. The children must be taught to hate sin, but at the same time scruples, anxiety and fear must not be aroused. They should detest sin and turn from it. This is a difficult task.

The teacher must know how to answer their problems, never to answer just anything, but always the truth. At this age, children should learn that there are two kinds of sin: original sin and their own actual personal sin. That is sufficient for the first notion. Original sin is washed away by baptism, and their own personal sins by the sacrament of penance. God loves them so much that He wants to take away their sins and make them holy.

The Commandments

Telling the children that each Commandment has two parts, as it were—one for grownups, and one for children—prevents anxiety about falling into mortal sin without knowing it, a fear which afflicts children sometimes. In order to help them, the Commandments should be presented as safeguards, not as prohibitions; they are not restrictions, but allow us to act freely, in security. One can compare the Commandments to the Rules of the Road. If they respect them, all goes well; if they do not, they will almost certainly have an accident. In the same way, the Commandments are for our protection.

It is certain that at this age the children are very curious, and they often ask how they came into the world. A holy priest, a Dominican, used to say that if children ask questions of this kind, they are ready for the true answer and capable of understanding it. But, he added, that great care must be taken to answer their questions only, and not to add further information that the child had not asked for. The more they ask at this age the better. They accept quite simply, without emotion and without embarrassment, the explanation given to them, and they are glad to know the truth. Later on, in adolescence, the children are not so simple, and this knowledge often causes them strong emotions and reactions.

What is Conscience?

It is necessary to tell small children what conscience is. They are so often told that conscience is a voice. But it is not a voice. The child, who takes things in a very matter-of-fact way, listens and hears nothing. Conscience is the soul, the intelligence, which makes us understand whether a thing should be done or not. Our soul does not give us any reason, but we know quite well that some things should be done or not done. Conscience must always be followed. God has put it in our soul, in our mind, to illuminate and to protect us, to keep us from sin.

The Sacrament of Penance

If we wish to go to confession three things are necessary: *First* of all, we must regret our sins, have contrition for them, as well as the firm purpose of amendment. This is most important because—though God is willing to forgive any sin, however serious, if we are sorry—He cannot forgive the smallest sin if we are *not* sorry. We must, therefore, ask God for the grace of true contrition.

Secondly: Our sins must be told to a priest because our Lord gave the priest power to forgive them. We should tell him everything. The priest will never speak of it. He will never be angry, shocked, or surprised. He knows all about sin. When we tell our sins with true sorrow, God forgives us.

The conscience of the child should always be respected. No one should ever ask him what he said in confession, nor should his confessions be laughed at. We should never say to him, "I hope that you said this or that." We must be ready to help him, but to speak to him in this way is quite another thing.

When children are taught about mortal sin, we should always speak of it as something that does not concern them; for it is rare that a child is able to commit mortal sin. They may have "material" for a mortal sin, that is, "grave matter"; but the knowledge and the malice are wanting or hardly existing. They are, therefore, not wholly culpable in God's eyes. It is best to teach them about mortal sin in relation to some imaginary criminal, who can have committed all the sins necessary to illustrate our teaching. It should never be taken as a matter of course that the children will one day commit mortal sin themselves.

Thirdly: We must make satisfaction. This means that if we have done something wrong, we must not only be sorry, but we must do something to make up for it, to repair it—just as broken things must be mended or replaced.

After our confession, the priest gives us a penance to do, usually a prayer to say. This is our reparation, a way of "mending" what we have broken. The prayer that the priest gives us, which we should say with love and attention, is part of our reparation, but it is in doing sacrifices of our own choice, and above all, in loving God greatly, that we make up fully for what we have done.

These are some of the ideas which help to strengthen the feeling of security in the child. The sacraments will heal the weakness that remains in the soul after sin. We should avoid telling the children all the time that God will punish them. Showing God as a severe and strict judge could easily frighten them. But they must be shown that every sin has a result, an effect in the soul, and also in regard to other people, and even with regard to the whole world. But God is there to help, to draw good out of evil.

Prayer

One of the most important things of all is to teach the children to pray. It is prayer that draws down graces on the soul. Through prayer a child gets to know and to love God as a real person. Children should be taught to live with God, to think of Him easily, and to speak to Him spontaneously, often, and of everything; in joy to thank Him; in trouble or suffering to ask for consolation and help; after a fall, for forgiveness. They have not very far to go in order to find God. He dwells there, in the depths of their soul—in His Holy Trinity—ever since they were baptized.

If taught along the lines we have briefly sketched out above, children should arrive—at the end of this stage of their lives—with clear, solid ideas, and with an ever-increasing confidence in the power, the mercy, and the love of God.

Religion should never, at any stage, be regarded as a school subject or an examination subject. It is one's whole life, a full-time job, filling every moment, day and night. The children must be sure of our Lord's love, His desire to forgive, His absolute forgiveness. They must believe in His power to put right what is wrong. This may take a long time, because of perverse human wills and intricate situations, but He can in His wisdom see the way out So we must pray and trust and sacrifice ourselves.

The Person who Teaches

We must remember that what is of utmost importance to the children of any age is the person who teaches. We must avoid teaching these things as if we had merely learned them by heart. Children must feel that we ourselves are absolutely convinced of their truth; and that the axioms and principles of our Lord are a part of our life. It is not only knowledge that we must give to the children, but the example of a sincere effort on our own part to live the Christ-life. One can never deceive children by an appearance of piety and virtue. Youth has a sure intuition of the sincerity or insincerity of our life. For those who teach this is the greatest difficulty. Did not our Lord Himself say that he who teaches—and does what he teaches—shall be great in the kingdom of heaven?

CHAPTER TEN

THE "MARIA MONTESSORI" SCHOOL OF RELIGION (ROME)

BY MARCHESA SOFIA CAVALLETTI

I t is an incontestable fact, to which we have borne and still bear witness, that children come with joy to their religious instruction; a fact which does not seem as natural to some people as to others. Most people think that it is necessary to attract children to religious instruction by means which are external to the subject itself, such as games, rewards, amusements of various kinds. We have established, on the other hand, that children come to us as to a feast; and often, after two hours fully devoted to lessons, it is still quite an effort to get them to go home. Recently a little girl, who had been summoned because her family had come to take her away, violently protested, saying: "They have come to take me away, already! They must have done it on purpose!" Very often I have heard the children, on arrival, make the following request to those who had brought them to school: "Please call for me as late as possible." In fact, we have known cases where mothers, and even fathers, have been condemned to interminable waiting for children who did not wish to leave.

One child, when she realized that certain difficulties had arisen which would have prevented her from attending the Course, burst into a flood of tears, which her grandmother was only able to assuage by assuring her that the obstacles would somehow be overcome. The parents of another child asked him, at the beginning of the year, what extra-scholastic activities he wished to continue, and he chose to keep up his religious instruction before anything else.

In general, most people would think that between gymnastics and religion the former would be more attractive to children, but they would be wrong. Recently I had occasion to summon a child—the lesson being over—telling him to hurry up as he had to go to his gymnastic lesson, and do you know what he replied? "Gymnastics can wait—can't they?"

One would think that television would be more attractive for children than religious instruction; but a boy, who lived in an environment which was anything but encouraging to piety, gave up for a whole year a special television program for children, because it coincided with the lessons in religion. I could go on for a long time giving examples like this. The children impatiently ask when Tuesday is coming round, or Thursday, the day of their lessons; and inquire, too, whether they will be allowed to continue coming after they have made their first Communion.

More than this, the religious lessons can be themselves used as prizes or means of enticement to things outside themselves. Thus one mother told her little boy that she would only continue to send him to our school, if he won the privilege by being good; and the little fellow had evidently made great efforts to behave well in order to come.

Heaven knows that we do not say all this to extol our work, convinced, as we are, that in all this it is little enough, or nothing at all. Our purpose is to give due recognition to the children, and to their judgment of true values. We do wrong to children if we imagine them to be so insensible as to prefer a gymnastic exercise to a liturgical function: No! "Gymnastics can wait," they have said so themselves. There is no necessity to "sugar the pill" of religious instruction with any games or other attractions; it suffices in itself, and *ad abundantiam,* to attract them more than any game or amusement one could invent.

Our Program

The children then come with delight, but what do they learn? It will not be out of place if we give some further explanations; especially as to how the lessons are carried on.

The lessons last two hours and always consist of a part which is explanatory; and a part which is given over to individual work by the children. The expository part is of course necessary; but it is to be noted that the real learning comes *after* the teacher's lesson; that is to say, when the pupil is able to think over and meditate upon what has been explained.

In this second stage also the child has need of our assistance, but this assistance does not now, however, come to him by means of further instruction from the teacher, but from the material. It is an aid toward a rethinking—a remeditating—on the part of the child over the precepts and principles in which he has been instructed.

Now a few words about our syllabus. It is our aim to plunge or steep the children in the very life of the Church, escaping from introductory forms of a vaguely naturalistic character. We are dealing with baptized children who have the right to live, to the fullest extent, the life of the faithful. And therefore it is for this reason, as will be seen, that a great part of our program is devoted to the study of the liturgy. Nevertheless this study cannot proceed separated from the Scriptures. Hence, in our school, the syllabus, mapped out for every grade (for we cannot here with propriety use the word class), consists of one part dedicated to the liturgy and another to the Holy Scriptures.

Within this general scheme the subject is graded in accordance with the ages of the children. We take into consideration three groups—the youngest from 4-5 years; then those who are preparing for their first Communion, from six years until they receive; and finally the children who have already made their first Communion up to their confirmation.

The First Age Group (4-5 years)

The smallest ones are introduced to the liturgy especially by means of knowledge of the sacred objects and vestments, with their names; and similarly with the liturgical colors, etc. They are also given exercises in movement which consist, for instance, in preparing everything that is necessary for the Mass, or for baptism; and also by participating in liturgical functions in an abbreviated form.

For example, the Easter liturgy is rich in elements which seem almost as if they had been made especially to attract the minds of children. One could mention in this connection the lighting of the Paschal fire—that fire which all at once shines out amid an environment of complete darkness.

These especially appropriate elements in the liturgy, i.e.,

especially suitable for this first age group, are isolated and enacted separately. While the somewhat older children carry them out, the smallest ones look on. So, now, when these children are conducted into the church they rediscover things with which they are already familiar; and thus are able to follow the liturgy in a most living manner. It is not a rare thing to find that, during these and similar exercises, there prevails an atmosphere of recollection which is most impressive. On one occasion we were performing the ceremony of the Easter candle. The boy who had the task of placing in it the grains of incense (in the form of a cross) was not yet seven years old, and found it difficult to insert the grains. Consequently the affair lasted rather a long time; but during the whole of that time there reigned an impressive silence.

The scriptural part of the instruction, for the smallest group, comprises the Creation of the world, special episodes from the life of Jesus, and certain parables. And here it is important to pay particular attention, because there are some parables which do not correspond to the mentality of this very early period. For example, the parable of the guest at the Wedding Feast who was turned out because he was not wearing a wedding garment is upsetting to the minds of the smaller ones. And the same applies to the parable of the Wise and Foolish Virgins. The wise virgins are judged to be bad because, having oil, they did not wish to spare any for those who had none. Before the age of six such moral problems do not really exist. Furthermore, the mind of the child, at this stage, is not yet capable of discovering that behind the fiction of the story, there is something else, and that this something is precisely the thing which is most important.

Suitable for this first age group are the parable of the Good Shepherd and the various parables in which Jesus explains the mysterious nature of the kingdom of heaven. I have never yet seen a child show signs of weariness at the relation—oft repeated—of these parables.

The Second Age Group
(From six years to the first Communion)

The second age group is composed of those who are being prepared for their first Communion, whose need, therefore, is to bear constantly in mind that Holy Communion is a sacrament and a sacrifice. It is necessary to initiate them into a general knowledge of the sacraments; and to a more particular knowledge of the Mass. The teaching of the Mass naturally presents itself as a more complex thing. One part of it consists of a real and proper study—made around the table—with the appropriate means at hand. This study—which is difficult to describe, but which can be seen by anyone visiting the school—is complemented in the succeeding years by a knowledge of the individual prayers of the Mass.

Another part of this study of the Mass consists, on the other hand, of exercises in movement by means of which the children are able to carry out themselves certain actions of the holy rite. The same method is used too in learning about the sacraments.

It is quite probable that some people might think that exercises of this kind could lead to an excessive familiarity with the sacred rites. This is not our experience. Last year, during the visit of a stranger, a group of children carried out the rite of baptism. At the end of it the visitor remarked that the little boy, who played the part of the priest, did not seem like a priest—he seemed more like a bishop, he was so serious! Moreover, when the children enact things of this kind they usually have—close at hand—a little model of a priest. This is done so that they will always keep in mind that what they are doing is only an exercise, while the real execution of the action belongs to the priest only. This is a point which must be made quite clear. They should not regard themselves as learning how to be priests themselves, but only as training themselves to be good laymen; and for this purpose it is necessary to know what is performed by the priest. A child is not able to understand a sacrament or a complex rite like the Mass simply by studying it in his head at his little table; it is necessary that he should go through the actions himself, one by one.

Learning and carrying out such actions, the children come little by little to an understanding of their mystical significance. Instead of going through the actions mechanically, the children acquire a real sense of the meaning of the sacraments. With the help of visible and tangible materials the words are fleshed out and a wealth of catechetical knowledge is provided which makes the most exalted concepts easy to understand.

In all this we are still on the plane of learning. But the central point of this liturgical study, and indeed the aim of all that we teach in our school, is a participation in the Mass, which shall be living and deep.

To this end there has been prepared a little missal which in its translation remains faithful to the text, but bears in mind that it is for the use of children. Therefore, it is in a language which is as far as possible both solemn and simple at the same time. This missal is introduced to the children gradually. This is made possible because the cover is fitted with a spring clip at the back, which permits the insertion of the prayers, by degrees, as the children are able to understand them. I am more and more convinced that the missal should be only used as a sort of class-book. That is to say that children should learn about the Mass in it *before* going to Mass; it is not necessary that they read it during the Mass. Mass is an action, and we make a continual *reading* of it.

The children must come to realize that they do not go to church simply to listen to the Mass, but to "make it," that is, of course, in those functions which pertain to the people of God. Thus, at their Mass in the Children's Chapel, it is the children themselves who prepare the altar furnishings, who read the Epistle and commentary and who—coming in procession together—bring their offerings up to the altar at the moment of the Offertory. So real and important to the children is this actual participation in the Mass that some children could not rest, on Saturday evening, until they had been provided with their offering to be given at Mass the next day.

Before they go to Mass they write, on a sort of diptych, the names of those persons for whom they wish to pray particularly; and then read them at the *Memento* of the Living and of the Dead. At the beginning of the Communion, they "prepare the table," spreading out the white "tablecloth" over the altar rails. All this makes the children's participation in the Mass a vivid experience; and more than one child has put the question to me, "Why does the Mass last so short a while?" Actually our Mass lasts almost an hour, and with the previous preparation an hour and a half.

Preparation for Holy Communion

We have special lessons for the children who are to make their first Communion. The subject of these lessons is, of course, Communion and confession. As for Communion we have found that the best preparation is to read and explain the prayers of the last part of the Mass, beginning with the *Our Father*.

Since the children have just entered the stage of being specially interested in moral problems the study of confession comes easily to them.

On the other hand what they do find difficult are the "evangelical counsels" taught in the Gospels. When one arrives at the stage of pointing out that one should not resist violence, that one should give way to the overbearing, then things become more difficult—even "too difficult" as a little girl once remarked. Then it is necessary to insist, to repeat and allow the children time to meditate upon and absorb such principles.

The foundation for this moral education consists naturally in the parables. We have initiated a sort of re-editing of the Gospel, in which every parable and every historical fact is contained in a separate little booklet. This renders it easier to read and brings it within the reach even of the smallest.

We have also found it a good plan that the children should be able to find, in their environment, the most important evangelical maxims synthesized in a lapidary or monumental form. To this end we have prepared a material which in its appearance brings to mind the ancient "Tables of the Law"—the Ten Commandments. For example, a child who is acquainted with the parable of The Unfaithful Steward will still find the Law of Pardon summed up in the maxim, "I will not pardon only up to seven times, but up to seventy times seven." Usually the communicants copy out these maxims on a scroll of parchment, which remains for them a memory of their first Communion.

The Third Group

The third group of children is made up of those who have already made their first Communion, and are therefore preparing for their confirmation. These go deeper into the study of the Mass, the sacraments, particularly baptism and confirmation. They also begin to acquire an elementary knowledge of the Bible, particularly the Psalms.

The synthesis of all that they have been studying up to now is contained in the Creed. In this connection the children prepare the "Story of our Salvation," which is true sacred history, the story of how God, through successive stages, guided humanity up to its redemption, and the founding of the Church which continues the work of Christ. When children have arrived at a certain stage they should come to realize that the history of humanity has developed according to the divine plan; that from the very beginning He has guided men to the knowledge of the one God, and His Law; how He has taught them an ever more elevated doctrine—through the preaching of the prophets—until the time when that light which had shone in the words of the prophets now in its fullness illuminated the whole world through the coming of Jesus.

Thus they come quite naturally to form the idea of God the Father and of His providence. From the establishment of this belief the passage is easy to the moral obligation that man has toward God—the necessity of sanctification and the duty of worshiping God through the liturgical means which the Church places at our disposal.

Thus in this last stage of their instruction the children rediscover all the elements which they have been learning from the first years; but now, however, they see them within the vast framework of the history of humanity, created by God, guided by God, redeemed by Jesus, and sanctified by the Church through the presence of the Holy Spirit.

How We Started

The school began almost spontaneously. The writer was requested to give some lessons on religion to a little boy, the son of a friend of hers; and this first child was quickly joined by three or four others. At that time we had no material; the children simply listened to a lesson and then made some drawings; that was all. It was only at one of the last lessons (we began in the month of March) that a Montessori directress—Gianna Gobbi—came, bringing with her a model of the altar and of the sacred objects and vestments used at Mass.

The enthusiasm of the children was suddenly tremendous. At the end of the first lesson a little boy began to cry because he had to leave. Another asked his mother if he would be able to come every day; and when she objected, since he would have to give up his music lessons, he replied, "This is more interesting."

So, with Gianna Gobbi, it was decided to begin a regular course in the following autumn. For that scholastic year we had about a dozen children. Now the number of our pupils exceeds sixty and another school of our type has been founded in a church in a modern part of Rome.

The publicity for our school has been carried out by the children themselves—who spoke about the religion lessons to their companions and friends.

The school consists of two classes and a little chapel. In one classroom are all the materials that have to do with the Scriptures, biblical geography and history—and there is a corner reserved for reading. In the other classroom there is the model altar with its furnishings, the model baptismal font with its requirements; the liturgical calendar; the scenes representing the principal episodes in the Christmas cycle, from the Annunciation to the Flight into Egypt (a sort of extended crib). According to the time of the year there is a similar set of scenes for the Paschal cycle. It is in this second classroom that the smallest children work, for the most part, but the divisions between the two classes is not a rigid one.

The little chapel is so arranged that the altar can be completely shut off from the rest of the hall—which can then be used for exercises which require greater space and liberty of movement.

Our lessons always take place in the afternoons and last about two and a half hours. The final half-hour is devoted to singing. The lessons always consist of an explanatory part, to begin with, by the teacher; the remainder of the time the children work individually.

Materials

Some of this has been copied from the Dominican Sisters at the Sion Hill Convent, Blackrock, Dublin—and from other material devised by members of the Catholic Montessori Guild in England.

Experience has shown us that for the parables it is helpful to have little wooden images representing the various people in the stories. With these one child carries out the action described in the Gospel, while another reads the text aloud from one of the booklets. Such figures are represented in a more or less abstract manner in order to differentiate them from the figures used in the Christmas or Easter panorama, since these latter stand for definite historical persons.

For the study of *Biblical Geography* we have prepared a plaster model of Jerusalem, in which the houses connected with the story of the Passion and of the Temple are movable. We also have a model of the Lake of Tiberias and our next model will be of the whole of Palestine.[14]

---

14   Cf. Chapter 11.

CHAPTER ELEVEN

"Living Holy Week"

How the Liturgy is Taught
at the Maria Montessori School in Rennes, France

BY M. AND F. LANTERNIER

M aria Montessori's thinking is universal. It is not addressed solely to Catholic or Protestant educators or members of any other particular religion. It is addressed to everyone whose intelligence is clear and objective enough to understand that all evidence points to the child as "the creator of man"—and that his right to this title must be respected.

On the religious plane the child is also the "creator of the man of faith." Dr. Montessori insists on the fundamental distinction, here, between the syntropic and entropic factors. The syntropic factor is the religious basis of man's nature, his need for spiritual activity and expression. It is found in all men, irrespective of their religion or degree of unbelief. The entropic factor is the element that has to be learned; it depends on education, but also on Salvation History which is not so much a creed, or a theological system provided by reason—as the biblical and evangelical Word which has been given to men by God continuously, in and through history:

the history of the people of Israel, the history of Jesus Christ and the history of the primitive Church.

Thus we can understand the value and scope of education provided by the liturgical cycle. It is through this liturgical cycle that biblical and evangelical history are manifest; it forces us to live and relive it; it reveals it to us and impregnates us with its truth—so that our lives are thereby transformed.

This truth Montessori calls *la Vita in Cristo*, Life in Christ. The Word of God was incarnate and lived our life, died on the cross and rose again on the third day so that we, too, might pass from the death of sin to the resurrection of our life as children of God. The mystery of the death and resurrection of the Christian in the death and resurrection of our Lord is taught us especially in the liturgical cycle of Easter (as Dr. Montessori has shown in her remarkable study of the liturgical calendar).

Although it is comparatively easy to convey the idea of Christmas to children, the mystery of Holy Week seems less accessible. Cribs and Christmas trees may be found everywhere, even in schools divorced from any concern with religion. Nevertheless one might ask if this crib, these fir trees—even when they are adorned with the symbols of Bethlehem—really convey any meaning, detached as they are from the context of Advent.

It has been suggested that the mysteries of Easter should wait until the children are more mature. What a misconception of a child's faith and understanding this is!

Holy Week

On the morning of Saturday in Passion week, at about 10:30 a.m., the children are assembled. Since they have already been prepared by the lessons of Lent, a simple proposition is put to them:

"Holy Week is the week in which Christians recall the events which took place during our Lord's last days on earth. We can consecrate this coming week to a living commemoration of it—or we can carry on with our schoolwork as if Holy Week had never taken place."

The unanimous answer which swells from the hearts of these children (rather than their tongues) is: "We want to *live* Holy Week!"

When one realizes that this response is entirely spontaneous on the part of true Montessori children, one understands that their enthusiasm is reminiscent of the episode in the Gospel—when the people in the Temple asked Christ to silence the children and He answered, "Upon the lips of infants and babies, you have composed a hymn of praise."

The Stage is Set

On Monday in Holy Week the work tables and chairs are set back against the walls. A great empty space is left. In this space the various historic sites are set up in the most authentic positions possible: Bethany, the house of Annas, the palace of Caiaphas, Herod's palace, Calvary, the Cenacle and the Garden of Olives. Finally in the center, on a table about fifteen feet in diameter, the Temple is put together. This comes in wooden sections which the children have painted in the art class and which has been built by a carpenter (the father of one of the students) according to a detailed blueprint.

All the children work together setting up the Temple, which has purposely been made as simple as possible—and this activity sets the mood for the days to come.

The Actors

In the midst of this setting are placed the actors; some 200 figures carved from wood are grouped in the buildings about the Temple and on the streets (see photo, p. 266).

These are the people who are mentioned in the Gospels—from the woman who anoints our Lord's feet to Joseph of Arimathea.

They are brought out, each in his turn—whether it is an actual person like the widow with her mite or a special social category like the Scribes or Sadducees, the Roman soldiers or the Temple servants. Each serves to clarify the events at once historical (incarnate in time) and mystical (i.e., eternal) in which Christ has been revealed to us.

The Action

What is actually taking place within this framework and with the use of these figures? According to the timetable in the annex which closely follows Father Lagrange's *Synopsis,* as far as the available time allows, the events of the Gospels are presented. Lagrange must be religiously adhered to—without invention, modification or addition. The children follow it all with implacable interest—even the most difficult passages of Tuesday's Mass or the discourse after the Last Supper.

To make everything completely comprehensible to the children what else is necessary? To embellish the dialogue between the various characters in such a way that they present themselves and what they stand for. Here, for instance, are the Sadducees who come to question our Lord about the resurrection of the dead. Before His appearance, it would be helpful to have them discuss the beliefs of the Sadducees, so that they will be fixed in the minds of our audience.

A change of pace is often called for. It is fine to characterize certain personages of the drama in comic terms—to show their purely political motivation or their inability to capture the mystic and transcendent aspects of what is taking place.

It will be readily understood that the actors in this drama play a microcosmic role. And that, especially from Tuesday on, if the direction has been competent, a whole town has come to life—whole social strata, ideas and men in action and reaction, all playing their historic role. So that, little by little, under the children's very eyes, the entire drama of the Passion stands revealed.

The Life of the Children Within This Framework

It is marvelous to watch how 120 children will organize their activities throughout the week. They form groups; some arranging the actors, others working on models and the scenery; there are those who read the appropriate passages from Lagrange and the Gospels; the smaller ones write the names of the personages involved in their workbooks or on the blackboard; those below the age of three participate only in the preliminary setting up of the Temple—they will not return before Easter Sunday. However, all those from four up share in commemorating Holy Week.

At the moment indicated in the Plan of the Day a signal is given—certain invariable notes on the piano or upon the bells—and suddenly from every corner of the school the children assemble around the directress. A passage from the *Synopsis* is read in its entirety; but it is also acted out by the children with the help of the wooden figures. A new world comes into being.

Some children remain in their places continuing their manual labors. If they seem indifferent to what is going on, watch more closely. From time to time an exclamation bursts forth which indicates with what rapt attention they have been following the reading. The smallest children crawl through the legs of their elders to get into the front row. Their wide open eyes, their attentive ears miss nothing.

Alumni come back for Holy Week, bringing friends; strange children glide in and out.

The Place of the Liturgy

One question remains: How does the liturgy dovetail into this drama—above all, what part does the liturgy of the new Easter rite play?

The transposition is made without difficulty. It is only a step from the episode of the "man with the pitcher," before the model which represents the house of the Cenacle, to preparation for the Holy Sacrifice of the Mass in the church where the liturgy of Holy Thursday will be celebrated. A directress who knows and loves children can bridge it with a simple remark.

And if the recitation of the *Synopsis* brings us to the Washing of Feet and the first Communion of the apostles as an integral part of the Last Supper, how easy it is to make this a truly living occasion—not by reading from the *Synopsis,* but by actual participation in the ceremony which the new liturgy calls the "Rite of Communion" at the hour of our Lord's Supper.

A devotion like the Way of the Cross becomes even more vital and profound to the children when it is enacted with the wooden figures. Thus they can hardly help appreciating our Lord's loneliness in the midst of this hostile mob.

Stations of the Cross

Finally I suggest that we next follow the children through Good Friday's Stations of the Cross. Adding to the regular ritual the deeply reverent recitation of the *Synopsis*—

consisting only of the Seven Last Words—an atmosphere of actuality is obtained that is almost impossible to describe.

The Stations terminate in the interment. The stone has been rolled against the entrance to the tomb. It is over. No further word is said. We depart. The earthly life of our Lord has been completed.

Holy Saturday

The older children will accompany their families to the evening devotions; and next day they will come back to school. Then, right away, the setting of the guards around Christ's tomb will strike the appropriate note. Although everything seems static, the actors are still on hand. Over there we see Annas; over here Herod; there stands Pilate at his judgment seat; there hangs Judas ... the crowd is everywhere. At Bethany life proceeds as before. But our Lord is no longer present . . . Jerusalem is a dead city.

The Easter Vigil

But the older children know very well that they will be invited to return at 11 p.m. for some mysterious event—of which no one talks but of which all are conscious.

A church has been chosen. The children go to it gladly, entering completely into the spirit of the liturgy.

First there is the mystery of the New Fire, and then of the New Water. After Mass is over they will each be given some of the new water; and each will light a taper from the Paschal candle, which will be carried, carefully shielding its flame, to school.

The Easter Vigil is over. The intense faith with which the children have participated in the rites is an indication of how well they have been prepared for it.

Easter Sunday

But what of the smaller children? They will join the rest at school at 11 o'clock on Easter Sunday.

They will find an entirely new decor. Instead of the purple veils over the flowerless altar there will be a scene that is all white and luminous. As sentinels before it stand the little tapers which were put there that very day. In their midst is the earthenware pitcher which holds the new water brought from the church.

Rising above it all is the Paschal candle, symbolizing the "Light of the World." Gleaming in the semi-obscurity of the background the cross remains, but it has been transfigured by the radiance of the Resurrection.

And then the Good News of the Resurrection is read—with all the human astonishment and incredulity that attended the original event.

The little candles are lighted one by one, to remind us of all that we have been through: the ashes, the Lenten examinations, fasting, and finally the illumination of the Paschal candle.

The Temple is shown there with its crowd. To leave it standing would be to fly in the face of history and take away something from the reality of our Lord's Resurrection. And so, leaping over several decades, the story of the Taking of Jerusalem and the Fall of the Temple is read. The walls tumble, the city crumbles and, amid their ruins, a large cross is raised—symbol of the eternal mission of Peter and Paul—and of their Church. That is the end.

☙—❧

Having seen the glow in all those young eyes as they reflect the LIGHT—having heard the joy in those voices chanting the ALLELUIA—we adults can achieve a special sense of the true joy of Easter.

PART THREE

CHAPTER TWELVE

THE ATRIUM: PRACTICAL SUGGESTIONS

I: THE ABSORBENT MIND

BY MARIA MONTESSORI

You must know that, in our schools, the life in the *Case Dei Bambini* is based on the small child's characteristics. And the most interesting and significant thing is that the small child has the power to absorb what is in his environment. This *Absorbent Mind* is a marked characteristic of little children. They just "take" without judging. *And what they take becomes a part of themselves—something which enriches their psychic life. This makes one realize that the child should be placed in a position so that he can absorb from the environment that which makes him grow.*

This fact is very important and very impressive and should be understood because, at this stage, the child takes spontaneously from his environment to construct himself; he possesses this power which later becomes lost.

This is our *Doctrine of Sensitive Periods*, the result of 40 years of observation and experience with children. The child, at this stage, has special sensitivities which lead him to absorb certain elements from the environment—and absorbing to transform himself. It is a creative work; the work of self-creation.

An Example: Language

The child takes in language from his environment *without a teacher*. But not only is he able to take in thousands of words, he transforms his vocal organs so as to reproduce them exactly. No adult can do it as well. In this way, as small children, we all came to possess our own language which is our "mother tongue."

The adult can learn a language with all its rules—but only and always *with an effort*.

"The Word Becomes Flesh"

The other day I saw a painting and underneath was written "The Word Became Flesh." Since I had been thinking about this mystery of learning a language, I took the phrase literally. This is what always happens with the education of children: "The word becomes flesh."

So the child masters this language in a way peculiar to childhood. He takes; he constructs; he makes himself grow to a man without effort or fatigue merely by living. It is the child who produces this creation.

So what the child "takes" *does* "become flesh" because language becomes incarnated in him. This is a matter of supreme importance: It is the *Period of the Absorbent Mind*.

We Must Begin Early

Hence we see how essential it is that religious education

should begin very early, in this period of the Absorbent Mind, and such instruction should be offered to the child who takes, who absorbs.

So it should be possible at this stage in the Atrium to put the younger pupil in contact with many things that have to do with religion: the Eucharist and the liturgical year; the sacraments, etc., *but in such a way that the child lives and acts; for his way of living at this time is to act and to do.* So we must give him a special environment—a special room furnished with prepared teaching materials which lead to action—as is done in the ordinary Montessori classroom. Let us summarize some of these:

Principles For Religious Teaching
1. It is necessary to have a special environment in which the religious life can develop—remembering that the child is a human being with the dignity of a human being.
2. This religious life develops by means of activity.
3. We must remember that the inner creative force in the child is much stronger than we usually think.
4. The teacher must endeavor to arrange things so that the child passes all his time in a religious activity.
5. Going from difficulty to difficulty and overcoming them. Each difficulty is presented in isolation through a manipulative material.

Further Notes on the Atrium

Though the Atrium is not a church it should be a room of special beauty, made in a semi-ecclesiastical style, with good lighting and attractive objects—such as statues, pictures, colored vestments—all well designed. It could have pointed windows which would, of course, be very low, down to the children's level; built like everything else in the room in proportion to the child's stature. There would be statues, here and there, of our Lord, His Blessed Mother, saints and angels—especially of the guardian angel. There is a particularly beautiful and striking statue of a guardian angel protecting a child from the approaches of a malign spirit in the Church of St. John Lateran in Rome.

Madonna and Child (Barcelona)

The regular Montessori exercises in movement, grace and courtesy lead naturally into the proper conduct in church. Above we see an Irish lass shining shoes. Below an English nun is explaining miniature brass models of altar furnishings. The children will spend hours polishing them—all the more cheerfully in honor of Jesus.

An Italian youngster pours water into the cruet with the same loving attention to correct physical movement. (Carlo is 5.)

Above we see an American girl scrubbing her hands with an almost ritual care. (Caterina is 6.)

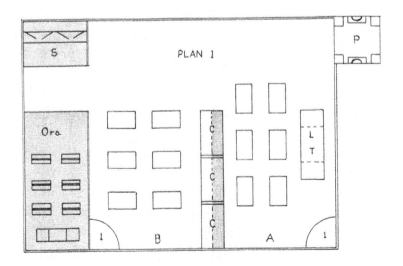

(A reproduction of this and many other famous statues can often be bought at Alinari Brothers, 100 Via Due Macelli, Rome.) The children would bring flowers to put in front of these statues and lights could be kept burning before them. Great use would be made of the walls of the Atrium which should be adorned with pictures illustrating Old and New Testament stories, the liturgical colors, Control and Error Diagrams, and so forth. Around the walls should be cupboards and shelves containing the various "occupations," which the children could choose from and work with, as in an ordinary Montessori class. There also could be a belfry tower with a bell that the children could use at certain times.

II: Notes On Plan I

BY THE EDITOR

These plans and notes about the Atrium are in no way intended to be slavishly followed. They are only put in here as suggestions and doubtless many readers would be able to improve on them.

This is a suggested ground plan of the Atrium, which is divided partially into two separate parts (A and B). The dividing partition (C, C, C) is composed of three cupboards which are taller man the cupboards at the side. They are mounted on casters so that they can be easily moved to the side in order to make one big room joining sections A and B together. This could be done when a story is being told or if the children are making a procession, rehearsing for a play, or at a singing lesson.

Room A is for the smaller children, ages 3 to 5, and the shaded cupboards in it contain more elementary materials—those of a more sensorial nature as, for instance, the liturgical colors, the early naming exercises in reading (putting names against objects), and also the various activities which have to do with L.T. (the Liturgical Table) of which more later. In this section (A) would also be carried out those exercises of a sensory-motor nature; such as, polishing the miniature sacred vessels, pouring water into the cruets, changing the water in the vases for flowers, and so on. In the corner of room *A-1,* where there is a quarter circle, could be placed a statue of our Lady with the Christ Child and in the corresponding corner in room *B-1* could be a statue of our Lord as the Good Shepherd.

Other Items In the Atrium

The rectangle in the corner marked Ora. is a little oratory similar to the one shown here. It has a small altar at one end and some half dozen little kneelers. This oratory is fitted up very much like a miniature chapel with the stations of the cross on the walls, holy water font at the entrance, and so on. Further possible details can be seen in the illustration of the actual oratory in St. Anthony's School, Mill Hill, London (see p. 254).

At the same end of the room (B) on the opposite side and shaded is S. S stands for a little sacristy with specially made cupboards and drawers for keeping the models of the sacred vestments and sacred vessels.

The Porch

The Atrium is entered through the porch, which is the ground floor of the belfry. It has two holy water fonts—one on each side.

Hooks for Clothes

Just inside on the right are rows of hooks for the children's clothes. As has been suggested, the children might don a special garment, when they come to work in the Atrium, over their ordinary clothes.

In a conspicuous place on the wall of the Atrium there could be a large reproduction of a picture of the incident described in the Gospel when the disciples tried to keep the little children away from our Lord and He exclaimed, "Let the little children come to me, and do not hinder them, for of such is the kingdom of God."

"The Best to the Smallest"

Montessori was always insistent that children should not be fobbed off with inferior art. On the question of providing them with pictures, she would have us make use of the wealth of illustrations provided for us by our great masters from the Byzantines to Rouault. She maintained that, though perhaps children are not able to put their impressions into words like an art critic, they are, none the less, very susceptible to the appeal of real beauty. We should never dream of putting them off with "pretty, pretty" pictures, or badly composed pictures, under the impression that as "it is only for children" any sort of illustrations will do. Child psychologists are agreed that the "explosive period" for appreciation of art takes place at about age five.

This applies, also, as far as possible, to the pictures we supply for the children to be used in their Time Lines, pictures for composition and so on. It is to be hoped that as this new approach becomes better organized, a collective effort will be made to pool experiences with the special aim of producing the kind of "activity materials" which have proved their practical value and efficiency with children.

Half A Loaf Is Better Than No Bread

We can imagine some reader saying: "All this Atrium business sounds very nice on paper, but I see no chance of it coming into existence in *my* school. We don't have enough room as it is to properly accommodate the children who come to our ordinary classrooms; much less, to be able to devote a special room to the teaching of religion."

We sympathize with this objection; and so we are anxious to point out that in any Montessori school one can do a great deal for the teaching of religion on Montessori lines *without having a special room for religion.* One can have the religious materials placed in the ordinary classroom on their own special shelves and cupboards just as you have the arithmetical materials together in one part of the room, and the materials for writing, reading and composition in another section and so on.

In one school I know they have made excellent use of a wide corridor for the religious materials. As you go down the corridor you see one section for keeping materials for the Mass, another for the Liturgical Year, another for the Commandments and so on. They have used the blind end of one corridor for making a very beautiful little oratory. The children come and get their materials from this corridor and either work there (it is a wide corridor) or bring the materials they have chosen into their own classrooms.

Counsels of Perfection

When one comes across Montessori's idea of the Atrium for the first time, it does seem like a "counsel of perfection"; but already many schools are beginning to adopt the idea— or at least work toward it. And as time goes on and new schools are constructed the idea will certainly be taken more and more into account in the making of the school plans.

It is not necessary, by any means, that a school must be a Montessori school in order to put into practice the idea of having a special room devoted to the teaching of religion. Though, of course, a school in which children are accustomed to choose their own work, and work freely and spontaneously by themselves, would make the running of any Atrium more easy.

The Atrium and the Work of the Parish

The difficulty at the present time is that the teachers have to prepare most of their own materials for the teaching of religion along Montessori lines. But already the situation is changing for the better. Some of the wonderful materials which have been worked out by the Marchesa Cavalletti in her school at Rome, are already being manufactured by a Roman firm. Other materials, e.g., for the teaching of the Liturgical Year, are also on the market in Italy. Without doubt, as the knowledge of this method spreads, there will be a great demand for such materials and the demand will create the supply.

One can reasonably look forward to the time when one will be able to order a whole set of religious materials including model altars and vestments, the Liturgical Year material, History Time Lines, Biblical Geography, etc., just as you can order the Montessori Sensorial materials, e.g., the materials for arithmetic, geometry, algebra, etc.

It is quite possible to envisage a time when these things will be used in CCD also. On Saturdays the parish hall could be turned into a sort of Atrium. The religious materials, kept in cupboards during the week, could be spread out on trestle tables and a group of children—thirty or more—of different ages could be set free to work at the materials (after having, of course, been previously initiated into how to do so). The younger section of the children could be at work with the materials—under a lay catechist—while the older children are receiving oral instruction; then, vice versa.

The children working at the materials in the parochial Atrium would do so either on other tables or desks; also, on other folding tables or on rugs on the floor—as children are constantly doing in the ordinary Montessori classrooms where the materials are such (e.g., Time Line) that they require a greater amount of space than an ordinary desk or table puts at their disposal.

III: NOTE ON THE MATERIALS USED IN THE ATRIUM

Whatever the subject—the Liturgical Year, the Mass, Biblical History, or Geography—with which we are dealing in the Atrium, by means of a material, there are certain rules or principles which we must follow:

1. *The Principle of Activity.* Visual aids, which have a definite value, are not enough for us. We must also have *Sensory-motor aids;* i.e., we must use a material which brings about an *activity* on the part of the child. "We are dealing with a child who has within him a principle of activity."

2. *It must be an individual activity,* which is directed by the will, bringing *mind and body* together in a functional unity.

3. This material must bring with it the *possibility of spontaneous repetition* which leads to self-perfection.

An Example: The Stations of the Cross

Suppose we are going to teach the *Stations of the Cross*. It would not be enough to give the child a book with the Stations in it. *We must prepare a material which leads to an activity*—something along the following lines:

1. We separate the pictures and mount each on a card.
2. We separate the reading matter—titles and captions.
3. We also separate the Roman numerals; mounting each on a card like the others, with the ordinary numbers on the back as a Control of Error. Then all these—groups of pictures, numbers and captions, kept separate by elastic bands—are placed in a box on the lid of which is written the *Stations of the Cross,* with, preferably, an illustration as well. So now we are ready for the individual activity by which the child will teach himself—true auto-education—by working with the materials in this way:

(a) He puts out the Roman numerals in a horizontal line on a long table or on a rug on the floor, thus:

I II III IV V VI VII VIII IX X
XI XII XIII XIV,

Or he could put them in two separate lines, as they are in a church:

I II III IV V VI VII
VIII IX X XI XII XIII XIV.

He uses, if necessary, the Control of Error—the Arabic numbers, which he knows—on the back of the card.

(b) Then he takes the pictures and places the corresponding Station under each Roman numeral. (Again there is Control of Error on the back.)

(c) Then he puts out the reading matter—headings and description—for each Station.

Then, after a prolonged individual activity, the work is finished. At first the child will probably refer to the Control of Error on the back of the card many times but—as he repeats the exercise, either on the same day or other days later—he will come to do it more and more without reference to the Control of Error, thus perfecting himself through repetition.

Not A Textbook

We wish to make it quite clear that this book makes no attempt at being a sort of practical textbook on Montessori materials for the teaching of religion—with or without an Atrium. This chapter and the two that follow it are merely in the way of what Montessori would call a *tentativo*—a sort of preliminary explorative attempt in the direction of a complete solution. Some day, someone will gather together all the various items of research which have been, are being, or will be made in this new field into an authoritative textbook. Meanwhile, with the view of helping those who would like to start right away teaching religion along Montessori lines and also with the intention of helping to pave the way for such an eventual textbook as mentioned above, we are putting before our readers some practical suggestions which have been found useful.

Dr. Montessori believed in teaching the sacraments by active participation. In the picture above an older girl is explaining the baptism materials to five-year-olds. (Rome.) Below a Spanish priest demonstrates the baptism ritual using a doll.

CHAPTER THIRTEEN

ON THE TEACHING
OF THE MASS

BY MARIA MONTESSORI[15]

*O Lord, may your sacrament fill us with holy fervor so that we
may delight in the celebration and grace of this sacred rite.*

THE POSTCOMMUNION FOR MONDAY IN HOLY WEEK

In teaching children about the Mass it is difficult to do so
all at once. It would be better to do this over a long period
of time and in the manner most suited to the possibilities
of the various ages through which the child passes. Thus,
at one epoch—the earliest—the senses and movement have
the greatest importance psychologically; and other means at
this epoch would not be within the child's comprehension.
So then the question might be asked: ought we to leave the
children in a state of complete ignorance about the Mass
until they are old enough to understand it—or should we
teach them what we can under the aspect of, and by means
of, the senses and movement?

We know that very small children have a special aptitude
to fasten on those things they learn through the senses and

---

[15] Taken from the Assumption College lectures —1940

movement. Therefore our aim is to create in the children who do them a sentiment of tenderness and love; and to impress on the minds of the *bambini* certain particular facts which will remain. In these representations, which they carry out as a sign of homage, they will move with delicacy and reverent silence, and in this way their little minds are brought to remember certain facts with a real devotion.

If at this precocious age we make use of the innate sensory-motor tendencies which characterize this epoch, at a later age the children will jump forward having already had a solid springboard.

This form of preparation is then a preparation of sentiment; because through the senses and movement, which are the vital factors at this age, knowledge of religion is absorbed in such a way as to stimulate and cultivate the corresponding emotions.

It might be objected: why should these things be done in the Atrium? Why not take the children into the church where everything is more beautiful? Our answer would be: in the *church* the children would not be able to carry out all these actions so slowly, so patiently, so exactly, so often and with such attention, as they would in a room set apart, and so furnished that they could carry out these actions with great deliberation.

The Teaching of the Mass—Second Period

Then there comes a second epoch in which children are interested in words and nomenclature and like to learn the names of a series of objects—a period which begins as the child approaches the age of five years, and is starting to read. At this period he likes putting out a series of objects and placing next to each a little card on which has been written its corresponding name. In fact, it is a genuine reading exercise.

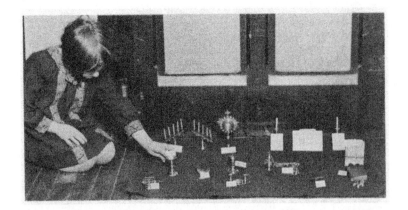

First steps in learning the Liturgical Colors.

Third Period

Later on there is a third period still more advanced in which the child is interested in, and able to understand facts about, the Mass on a higher plane. For these too we must prepare special means, which like all our didactic materials solicit an activity which can be carried on alone and spontaneously by the children, once they have been taught their proper use. How long they work with any particular material is not for us to say; the child himself knows better than we do when he has reached "saturation point."[16]

So in this way—to sum it up—we should not wait to begin teaching children about the Mass (and other religious

---

[16] See *Maria Montessori: Her Life and Work*—"The Inner Guide," p. 269

matters) until they are "of age." We should seek how to do so at every period of their lives—following different forms of instruction, which correspond to those three differing epochs. Examples of such materials are dealt with later on.

The Liturgical Colors

Small children, who are in a sensitive period—for all that has to do with the senses—show at this stage a great interest in colors. In the Montessori class they have already been introduced to the color tablets. So then, carrying out the idea of "supernaturalizing" the natural, they should now be introduced to the liturgical colors and will show a corresponding and even greater interest in them. This can be done in various ways:

1. We could have large strips of the liturgical fabrics hanging, like tapestries, on the wall; one set longer for the Easter cycle and one set shorter for Christmas.

2. *By Comparison of Textures:* In the ordinary Montessori school the child learns to distinguish by touch fabrics of different textures. In the Atrium, there would be two sets of fabrics—but these would be the materials from which the liturgical vestments are made. For the feasts of Christmas and Easter there are fabrics of a special beauty and luster. These two sets could be compared by touch and sorted with that exactness which is so important at this stage.

3. *The Liturgical Table:* There should be a special table kept in one place in the Atrium which could be used as a *"Liturgical Table."* To go with this table there could be a set of different tablecloths—each made of a particular liturgical color. And every day—as a matter of course—children would spread out on the table the

cloth of the color of the Mass of that day or period of the year. Not a great deal would be *said* about it; it would be a thing to be done and seen. If there is a garden, flowers which have the liturgical colors could be planted and cared for. And there could be a set of little vases similarly colored. On each day flowers and vase and the liturgical tablecloth would be put on the table of the color appropriate to the day. Artificial flowers could be used. Thus children living in this environment would—even at this early age—grow up accustomed to the fact of the liturgical colors. This they would see against a sequence of days with the same ferial colors and then the sudden appearance of a white tablecloth (e.g., Nativity of the Blessed Virgin) or a red tablecloth (as at Pentecost or the feast of a martyr) would make a deep impression.

Material for the Liturgical Colors

For the older children, who by now can read, there would be other materials for the teaching of the liturgical colors.

One such material would be as follows: five cards would be set apart and on each would be one of the liturgical colors. It would be best to have a piece of the actual cloth mounted on each card. Then a large number of little tickets or labels would be made with the names of the various Sundays in the year and the chief feast days—such as Christmas, Easter, Pentecost, Feast of the Sacred Heart, the Assumption of our Lady, and so on. The exercise to be done by the child would be as follows. All cards are placed in a line with a space below them. Then the child takes, at random, the labels or slips with the names of the various occasions—the feasts, etc.—and places each under the appropriate card.

VIOLET	WHITE	GREEN	RED	BLACK

The Control of Error

On the walls there would be a diagram of the liturgical colors and the particular occasions on which they are used. This serves as a key or reminder and could be consulted in doubt. Or the Control of Error could be made by putting a daub of the corresponding color on the back of the label with the Sunday or feast day written on it.

PREPARATION FOR MASS: THE ALTAR

In the last section we took up the liturgical colors and the various sensorial-motor exercises. Now we will concentrate on something more important. Our aim is to show how we can make even very small children understand what the altar is, or represents.

We shall do this, *not* by oral teaching but through an activity. The Atrium would have special furniture in it and included would be the following:

1. Twelve little stools, very simple and severe in style (like prisms).
2. A small armchair.
3. A table which is so constructed that it can be made shorter, by having the two ends hang down on hinges when the supporting struts are folded in.
4. White tablecloths (three as on altar).

How to Begin

We begin with exercises similar to those in our ordinary Montessori school. There they are given lessons in moving chairs and tables silently from one place to another. Here the children are taught to move this liturgical furniture gracefully—without any noise—and they learn to put each piece in its proper position.

The table and stools are set along the wall. The armchair is in the middle of the table between it and the wall with a small crucifix behind it. It is the same table we mentioned before, on which on other occasions we place tablecloths with the liturgical color of the day. So then it is a special table. But today we are doing a different exercise. The children will take the twelve little stools placing six on one side of the armchair and six on the other around the table, doing it very quietly and precisely. At first, then it is just an exercise of exactness to know how to place and replace the stools.

The Little Vestments

Another means to the end we have in view is to have the children put on vestments—white vestments adorned with ribbons of different colors.

1. One has a red ribbon.
2. One has a green ribbon.
3. One has a dark violet ribbon.
4. The others have white ribbons.

So then we choose thirteen children to take part in a little drama. The one with the red ribbon stands for our Lord; the one with the green ribbon—symbolical of hope—stands for St. Peter, the first pope; the one with the dark violet ribbon stands for Judas. These little details do not give much information but they are important to fix certain points in the mind.

Thus we have so far:

1. The table with armchair and stools to place and replace.
2. Little vestments and ribbons.
3. Certain special people.
4. The number thirteen.

Then comes the exercise for the children who take their seats on the stools; six on each side of the armchair with its occupant wearing the red ribbon. After the children have done this same exercise a good many times and know how to do it perfectly, later they can add to it by placing a white tablecloth on the table, and when that is done a chalice and a plate.

So, up to now, we have had these little scenes of activity—and they bring to our minds certain items: the table, the twelve apostles, our Lord, bread and wine.

The Explanation

The directress can now collect the children together and explain to them that what they have been doing happened before on a very special occasion. That was when the table was made ready for the Last Supper which Jesus and His disciples took together in a house in Jerusalem. She explains briefly, without going into a lot of detail, that some wicked men put Jesus to death on the cross and that one of these wicked men—Judas—was one of our Lord's own apostles. He was the one with the dark violet ribbon.

How Much Should We Teach Small Children About the Passion?

I am sometimes asked: Should we teach small children the story of the Passion? I would answer: It depends. Catholic children are born with the crucifix in front of them and as they grow up they see it everywhere—in the church, in their homes, in pictures and on rosaries. Now at this early age, as we have often said before, children "absorb" what they find in their environment, but unreflectingly, without forming judgments about them.

So for this reason when the directress tells them, at this stage of scenic representation, that Christ was crucified they accept it normally. But with non-Catholic children the case may be very different

It might be said that the Last Supper is too significant and complex for preschoolers to handle. I would insist, here, that at this stage we are chiefly involved in action, rather than explaining. The action will have its reverberating effect.

In the Atrium the children carry out these exercises with a special dignity, more easily than in any ordinary classroom. For in the Atrium there could be certain colors in the windows (better still, stained-glass pictures). This would add a more solemn atmosphere to the room, as the children slowly and silently approach the table. Or they could do it, with curtains drawn, by candlelight; the older ones carrying lighted candles (handling things carefully, e.g., a full glass without spilling a drop, or a little bell without letting it ring—part and parcel of the exercises they have already done in the ordinary Montessori class).

So then, to return to our dramatic representation. After the teacher has told the children the story of what happened—up to our Lord's death—she would summarize the situation by saying that Jesus is dead and that one of the apostles, who is also dead, was the cause of His death. Therefore, two persons are missing. So now we have only the children with the green and white ribbons left.[17]

Now a new phase in the little drama begins. The ends of the "liturgical table" are now let down and the table thus made smaller to look more like an altar. Several of the children,

---

[17] It seems rather hard on the child who has played the part of Judas to be excluded from the further development; so we would suggest that the same child could now take a white ribbon and represent Matthias, the new twelfth apostle—although actually he was not elected by the Twelve to take the place of Judas until afterwards. *Editor.*

instead of just one, come up to prepare the table. As they do this they put on *three* tablecloths as on the real altar, one of which hangs down at both ends.

Another change is this: whereas on the former occasions the armchair had been placed in the middle facing the child representing our Lord, there is now placed a crucifix on the table in the middle.

The chalice and bread are now brought in and put on the table, but covered up with a veil as if, our Lord being dead, there was no more use for them.

While this is going on the other children stand around solemnly and look on. It all seems very sad.

The other children—those not acting in the drama—could tie a black sash around their waists as a sign of mourning for our Lord's death.

Then they could all join in a procession—the "actors" walking first—singing a hymn of mourning.

The procession over, the "actors," led by St. Peter with the green ribbon, go up to the altar and place their chairs in a row in front of the shortened white altar with St. Peter facing them in the middle of the table on the opposite side.

ഔ—രു

Editor's Note: Our manuscript of Montessori's lecture from which the above was taken, comes to an end at this point—except that she adds the following concluding remark: "Our aim in all this is to give these little children the impression that the altar which they have often seen in the church is really the same thing as the table which was used at the Last Supper; and that the things which are done at the altar are a record, even more, a *continuation of what took place at the Last Supper.*"

This being so, we are confident that Montessori would never have allowed the actors of these "representative scenes" to remain forever in a state of despondency on account of our Lord's death. She would certainly have completed them with another scene in which the sadness was dissipated by the news of His glorious Resurrection. In fact, Montessori herself implies as much in the phrase underlined just above—"a *continuation* of what took place at the Lord's Supper."

In some way or other an attempt ought to be made—for the sake of the children—to have them act a scene in which this change from sorrow to joy could be portrayed. In whatever way we did it we should bear in mind what Montessori says above, that these little scenes aim at evoking a sentiment *through action* rather than through words and intellect.

When the last scene, as described above, has been carried out a number of times, and perfected, the directress one day could call the children together again and make a second and further explanation. She could tell them in simple terms how our Lord, after being put to death and buried, rose again triumphant and alive from the tomb on the third day; that He is still alive and will remain *alive* forever more and forever with us: "I shall be with you until the end of time."

And how does He do this? At a certain moment, when the priest is saying Mass, our Lord comes down from heaven to the altar where He is really and truly present just as much as He was at the Last Supper. We cannot see Him because He hides Himself under what looks like bread and wine.

He does this because He wishes to come to each one of us in Holy Communion, as our special Friend and Savior. So there is no need for us to be sad any more, because Jesus is alive again—and will be alive forever.

To act this out the children would carry out the little drama (as described above), in which the whole atmosphere was one of sorrow and sadness. The scene could end up with the child representing St. Peter at the middle of the altar, facing the other children sitting on their stools.

Then at a given moment another child—dressed as an angel—could come in, and go straight to St. Peter. At his appearance all the children would kneel. When the angel reaches St. Peter he whispers something in his ear—and then departs. "St. Peter," his face all smiles, gets up and goes to the first child at the end of the line and whispers something in his ear. He, in turn, smiles and claps his hands with joy, and passes on the good news into the ear of the next child, who responds in the same way—and so the glad tidings are passed on (children love telling a secret) to the end of the line. Then all the children could get up and go to a side table, take off their black sashes of mourning and put on white or gold ones. This done they could make a joyful procession around the room, singing a glad hymn and perhaps expressing their jubilation in a dance.

The procession would pass by a table on which were placed blessed candles; and as each child passes it he could take a candle and proceed toward the altar with it.

Meanwhile, St. Peter, at the altar, has uncovered the chalice and the paten with the bread. Then he places a statue of our Risen Lord in front of the crucifix (which has already been placed on the altar—see above) and puts the chalice and bread on each side of the statue.

He also places two candelabra—like the ones used at Benediction—at the ends of the altar. Then the procession approaches the altar; each child carrying a candle. These are placed in the candlesticks either by the children or St. Peter—who lights them.

When all is ready, St. Peter, who might have a small thurible to use, and all the children (behind him) in one or two rows kneel before the altar. There could be a concluding hymn.[18]

---

[18] The children might also re-enact the Jewish Passover meal which the Last Supper actually was and from which our Mass originates.

The Model Altar and Its Equipment

Some Suggestions on How it Can Be Used

One hears a great deal these days about the educational value of visual aids; for, as the poet says, "Things seen are mightier than things heard." But the more one understands the psychology of the Montessori Method the more clearly one comes to realize that for children visual aids are not enough; they also require sensory-motor aids.

Suppose you wish to teach children about the Mass, the altar and its appurtenances and their uses. Well, first you could simply talk about it. Next you could talk and illustrate your lesson with pictures, which would be better. Better still, would be to have a set of miniature models—altar, chalice, paten, burse, candles, vestments, etc., and after describing them, show the action. And then allow the children to handle the objects, name them and go through the actions themselves. We give below two accounts taken from our own observation in two different schools, which indicate practical ways in which the models can be used.

A Collective Lesson With A Model Altar

The lesson described below was given to a class of a dozen or more children, who were gathered in an informal group around the teacher and the altar. It took place in one of the rooms in the Dowanhill Montessori School, Glasgow, Scotland, which is run by the Sisters of Notre Dame de Namur. It is only fair to add that it was not a specially staged lesson, but just part of the ordinary school routine at which, without any warning, the editor was permitted to be present. On a table near the model altar were spread out models of the various sacred vessels and vestments used by the priest

Miniature altar (Rome)

in the celebration of Mass. The average age of the children was about eight years. The lesson, by the way, was given by a lay teacher, who seemed to be just as interested as the children themselves. We have recorded the lesson in the conversational form in which it was given.

Directress: This morning the priest is wearing white vestments, because it is the Commemoration of our Lord's baptism. On what days does the priest wear white?

Kathleen: On the feasts of our Lord and our Lady.

Directress: Any others?

Joyce: Of the saints who are not martyrs.

Directress: Yes, also on the feast of the Holy Angels. *(The directress chooses a white chasuble from among the others and holds it up.)* Now who can tell me what the color white signifies?

Cicely: It is to show purity and innocence.

Directress: While we are talking of colors, who can tell me on what day the priest wears a red vestment?

Cicely: On the feasts of the holy Martyrs.

Directress: Any others? *(Pause)* Also on the Feast of Pentecost. What other colors does the priest wear?

Margaret: "Violet.

Directress: When does he wear violet?

Margaret: During Lent.

Directress: At any other time?

Cicely: During Advent.

Directress: Are those all the liturgical colors used?

Several: No, Miss . . . black and green.

Directress: When is black used?

Margaret: At Masses for the dead.

Directress: At any other time?

Mary: On Good Friday.

Directress: Very good, and when is green used?

Joan: On all the other days which are not special feasts.

Directress: Who can tell me which vestments are changed according to the different feasts and times of the liturgical year?

Joyce: The chasuble, the stole and the maniple.

Directress: We must not forget the tabernacle veil, the chalice veil, and the burse. Now who would like to lay out the vestments which the priest uses for Mass? *(All hands go up eagerly.)* Well, Joan, you may try. *(Joan takes up the chasuble.)*

Directress: What is the name of the vestment which you have in your hands?

Joan: This is the chasuble.

Directress: Of what does the chasuble remind us?

Mary: Of our Lord's words: "My yoke is sweet, my burden light."

Directress: The next one, Joan. *(She picks up the alb.)*

Joan: This is the alb.

Directress: What does that represent?

Margaret: It is to remind us of the purity which the priest needs to celebrate Mass worthily.

Directress: Now the other things. *(Joan picks up the amice, cincture, stole and maniple and their significance is explained.)* Will somebody arrange them in their right order—as the priest will want them when he puts them on? *(This is done.)* As the priest puts on the garments, he says a special prayer with each. Do you see that little cross on the amice? What does this remind us of?

Mary: That the Mass is the same Sacrifice as that of the Cross.

Directress: When the priest puts on the amice he kisses the cross on it and touches his head with it.

Besides the priest's garments, what other things must we get ready? *(Forest of hands again.)* Margaret?

Margaret: The chalice and the other things for the altar.

Directress: (as Margaret takes the next object) What is that?

Margaret: It is the purificator.

Directress: What is that used for?

Margaret: To wipe the chalice.

Directress: Now the next thing. What is the paten for?

Cicely: It is for the host to rest on. *(The chalice veil and burse are taken out and named at the same time.)*

Directress: What is in the burse?

Cicely: The corporal.

Directress: Take it out, and look at it. The name comes from the Latin word *corpus*—a body. It is so called because it is the cloth on which the Body of Jesus is going to rest. The priest may not put down the chalice or the host on the altar unless the corporal is there.

Now we must get the altar itself ready. Kathleen, won't you do it? The first thing is to fold up the cloth which is on the altar at present. *(This is done.)* What do you see on the altar?

Kathleen: A square stone.

Directress: What is it called?

Joan: The altar stone.

Directress: Quite right, and the altar stone is vital to the altar; what do we mean by that?

Kathleen: A priest cannot say Mass except over an altar stone.

Directress: Yes. For instance, if a priest wanted to say Mass in a private house—as he does sometimes—he must take an altar stone with him, and it must have been blessed by a bishop.

What is there in the middle of a real altar stone?

Cicely: Some relic of the saints.

Directress: Where do the relics come from?

Mary: From Rome.

Directress: From the catacombs at Rome. In the catacombs, as you know, most of the early martyrs were buried; there the Christians used to meet together for worship; and there, too, the priests would say Mass. For an altar they would use a tombstone under which was buried one of the martyrs. That is how the custom of saying Mass over the relics of the martyrs began, and it has been kept up from that day to this.

What else is there on the altar that originated in those times?

(Pause.) Well, you must remember the catacombs were under the ground and therefore quite dark.

Several: Oh, the candles!

Directress: Yes, there must always be at least two lighted candles during Mass, and this is to remind us—among other things—of the times when the persecuted Christians were obliged to hear Mass in those underground passages. Even now, when visitors go to the catacombs in Rome—which happens every day—before they go in, each is presented with a candle to light up his way. Now to go on with the preparation of the altar. What is the first thing to put on the altar?

Ruth: The altar-cloths

Directress: How many are there?

Ruth: Three. *(These are put on the altar.)*

Directress: Why are there so many altar-cloths? *(No one knew).* It is out of reverence, lest some of the drops of our Lord's Precious Blood should fall from the chalice. Then they would not go through on to the altar beneath, but would be caught by the cloths. And if any drops did go through on to the altar-cloths, the priest himself would have to wash them out.

(Pause.)

Directress: And now what is this little table called?

Cicely: The credence table.

Directress: What must we put on it?

Cicely: The cruets with the water and the wine. *(The cruets are placed on the table.)*

Directress: What else?

Joyce: A little towel and a small basin for the priest to wash his hands. *(These are put on.)*

Directress: (looking around) Now is all ready? We have forgotten something which should be on the first step leading up to the altar; what is it?

Several: Oh, the bell! *(It is placed in position.)*
Directress: And here is the priest's hat. What is it called?
Mary: A biretta.

Directress: Now let us imagine that Mass is just going to begin; and we shall go through all the actions of the Mass, and see exactly what the priest does and why he does it. *(She is about to begin, when a bell rings.)* But it will have to be another day, for it is time to stop now.

Lesson With A Model Altar: Second Example

Very different was the school and the general conditions in the next example we give of the way in which a model altar can be used. It was in a primary school in a slum district in Dublin, run by the Sisters of Charity. There were fifty-six children in the class—average age about 6-7—and Sister Mary had to cope with them all alone. The class was run on Montessori lines as far as Sister Mary was able to do so with the limited means at her disposal. (I noticed that a child, who was working out her tables on a Montessori multiplication board, was using dried cherry stones instead of the usual red beads, and many other ingenious substitutes which would have horrified orthodox Montessori teachers.) But the spirit of Montessori was certainly there, and the children were all busy working away *individually* with great gusto. Some twenty of them had taken their chairs and tables into the small playground where they all worked with surprising concentration and self-discipline. Some of the children were busy at little household jobs, some with sensorial materials, others with the elements of "The Three R's"; but what interested me most that morning was something that was going on near the windows.

Two little girls were going through the whole action of preparing an *altar for* Mass. The school harmonium, turned back to front, did duty for the altar. The various objects required had been put on a little table by the Sister in charge. With a quiet and dignified efficiency, which was very pleasant to behold, the two children set to work. First came the altar-cloths, three of them; then the candles, tabernacle, crucifix, Missal-stand, altar-cards and so forth. After that there was a great preparation of the chalice and its appurtenances by one of the children while the other got ready the credence table. They did everything by themselves, not once did the teacher intervene.

I noticed with interest, however, that one of the little girls corrected the other several times; once to point out a mistake in the order of the altar-cloths and once to say that the purificator came before the paten. They knew the names, too, of the sacred objects—both in English and Gaelic.

The chalice and the candlesticks were made of wood gilded over, and cost very little. In fact, they cost the school nothing at all, as they were made by the nun's father, whose hobby is woodwork.

Snapshots give a very inadequate idea of the way in which the children worked. One would really need a movie-camera to portray the quiet precision and graceful actions of the children and their serene enjoyment of their work. It was clear they had understood the whole process of preparing for the Mass down to the most minute detail, in a way which could never have been theirs had they simply listened to a description or merely watched another doing it.

"But what about all the other children of the class while this was going on—what were they doing? Such a method would be all right if you only had a small class, say, of a dozen children."

Well, let me tell you, Sister Mary has 56 children in her class, and still she is able to do it. That is the wonderful thing about the Montessori Method. Each of the other children was busy in the same way; not, I mean, doing the same thing, but busy with some similar sort of occupation, i.e., involving this double activity of hand and brain.

Some were sweeping the floor; others washing out dishrags, or their own handkerchief; some were watering the plants; others were doing sums of various sorts (with bead bars for numbers); some were matching pictures with words (in Gaelic), others again doing various forms of drawing and coloring, but *all* actively engaged and, therefore, all concentrated, quiet and disciplined.

Though Montessori began her work over 50 years ago, it is surprising how long it takes this principle of teaching through activity to sink into the minds of teachers. If they are Catholics they ought to be quicker than others to appreciate it, for the Catholic Church, in its practical wisdom, has all along made use of the same principle.

And yet we continue year after year to deny these small creatures the necessary foundation for their mental growth. We are worse than that Pharaoh who denied the children of Israel straw for their bricks, for we oblige these poor mites to build without bricks at all.

And then we complain they are lazy, inattentive, noisy and disobedient. Yet the construction upon which they are engaged is one which will be greater and more lasting than the pyramids. For, when you come to consider it, the main task of childhood—what is it but the construction of that human personality which will last *in saecula saeculorum*.

The following story appeared in the Seattle *Progress* on February 22, 1963:

For all you parish guild members who search for a practical and worthwhile project each year, take heed of the ladies of St. Gerard Guild in St. Matthew Parish who have just completed a junior-size altar and vestments for the use of the school children in their study of the Mass.

Using everything from a glass goblet to the top of a silent butler, the ladies, under the direction of Mrs. Gino Tedesco, guild president, and Mrs. Edward Terhar, project chairman, have fashioned a complete altar as well as two sets of priest's vestments—10-year-old size.

All items were checked by Rev. George Rink, assistant pastor, to make sure they were liturgically correct and Rev. Walter J. Mortk, pastor, donated the Mass cards and candles for the altar.

The Mass cards were reduced in size by photostatic process and encased in plastic.

The tabernacle is a brass-colored can used by bakeries for eggwhites. Doors and hinges on the tabernacle were welded by Ray Boulet and the mahogany altar was made by a former parishioner, M. Bullock. Husbands of guild members made the candlesticks and did the necessary spraying and painting.

A plastic saucer from a child's tea set was sprayed gold for the paten and the Communion paten was fashioned from the top of a silent butler welded on a wooden handle and sprayed gold.

The chalice was a ruby-red goblet sprayed gold and the Missal-stand was a wrought-iron stand to hold a cook book. A piece of fiberglass used in a decorative screen was made into the altar stone.

One guild member wove the cinctures for the vestments on a spool knitter. Although there are now two sets of vestments, one white and the other green, a purple set will be finished in time for Lent and all are made of raw materials. Guild members were able to borrow patterns for most of the vestments but for some vestments they had to do their own pattern drafting.

The entire project was presented to Sister Irmalita, St. Matthew school principal, at special ceremonies at the school last week. It will be used by all eight grades as well as the CCD classes.

The Work In the Atrium Should Be Misso-Centric

In her mystical *Drama of the Mass* (as yet unpublished) Montessori makes it clear how, in the first century, after the death and Resurrection of our Lord, "the new religion

developed around the Last Supper and its continuation in the Holy Eucharist." In a similar way she would have the Catholic child's own individual growth develop from the beginning around the Mass.

We have already pointed out that she recognizes a first period in which the little child is able to absorb many matters in a sensory-motor way, and that this sensibility is made use of in various ways; in learning of the "Good Manners Required in Church"; in arising and sustaining an interest in the liturgical colors; in the enacted scenes to show that the altar is really the same thing as the table of the Last Supper, and so on.

Then we saw how, as the child's mind develops and he begins to read, the directress provides him with reading activities, many of which are centered around the objects used in the Mass and the Ecclesiastical Year.

"Later," she says, *"there is a more intellectual stage in which he is able to comprehend more fully what the great drama of the*

Mass really signifies. This presents a vast field of culture, for the Mass not only represents a synthesis of our religion, but also of the whole psychology of man. In fact, to follow the Mass properly requires a man to make use of all his energies—physical and spiritual—that is, to follow it with body and soul."

All School Subjects Should Focus On the Mass

Far from religion being treated as a subject apart we should so arrange it that everything which the child learns— his general instruction and culture—should be used to illuminate the great Sacrifice of the Mass.

Take geography, for instance. The child has been learning how the earth rotates on its axis once every 24 hours, thus bringing about the phenomenon of day and night. This brings home to us the fact that day is always dawning at some part of the earth; and with the dawn the Church, with its bells, summons Christians to assist at Holy Mass.

Furthermore, the child learns that the earth, in its annual course, moves around the sun. This, too, is a matter which has a direct religious significance; for during the solar year, as the seasons come and go, so also do the seasons of the liturgical year. These bring to life, as they come, the memory of events in the life of this God-Man, who descends among us every day.

It is interesting also to realize that we have to find out with precision the exact position of the heavenly bodies in order to determine, each year, the date of Easter, and with it many other feasts. In this manner the Mass is put in rapport with the universe and takes on a cosmic significance.

In a similar way, the study of history can be brought to bear on the Mass, because (as we shall see more clearly in the next chapter) as the child puts out the Time Line, the Last

Supper with its continuation in the Sacrifice of the Mass, is visibly seen to form the central point in human history—the moment of transition from the Old Testament to "the New and Eternal Testament—the Mystery of Faith."

The study of art can also be made to focus on the great religious events which are the foundation of our Catholic faith. All down the centuries works of artistic genius have been created which bear upon the life of our Lord and the history of the Chosen People. The more advanced children would be interested in the comparison of those two great masterpieces by Raphael—one depicting the Sages and Philosophers of Pre-Christian time, and the other showing the great saints of the Church, gathered round the monstrance from which our Lord continually reigns on earth. There is great scope for a combined study of religion and art in this field; and files could be kept and collections made as time goes on, thus developing at the same time a more just appreciation of good art, with a deeper reverence for the Divine Person who has been, and still is, its constant inspiration.

The Liturgical Year

We shall not in this book attempt to discuss Dr. Montessori's ideas on the teaching about the ecclesiastical or liturgical year. She herself has written a little book on the subject entitled *La Vita in Cristo*; and it is hoped that before long this will appear in an English translation.[19]

Meanwhile, we suggest making the following materials.

---

[19] For those who can read Italian, we might mention that this book—as well as *La Santa Spiegata ai Bambini* (The Holy Mass Explained to Children), can be procured from the St. Leo Bookshop, Box 577, Newport, R.I. *La Vita in Cristo* can also be purchased in its French translation from the St. Leo Bookshop, included in a book entitled *L'Education Religieuse* by Montessori—published by Desclee de Brouwer of Paris.

First Material: A Comparison between the Solar Year and the Liturgical Year.

Two circles of the same size are cut out in cardboard or plywood. The first is divided into four equal parts, or quadrants; they represent the four seasons of the solar year—spring, summer, autumn and winter. Each segment should be colored; winter, white; spring, green; summer, yellow; and autumn, brown (or whatever color is preferred).

The exercise consists in putting together the four parts to make the circle; then putting on these four sections their names on little labels. An arrow must also be placed to show which way the year revolves in the diagram. Finally the child puts a yellow or golden disc in the center to represent the sun, around which the solar year revolves.

The second circle represents the liturgical year, with its main divisions or seasons. Here we notice that there are really only TWO SEASONS—the Christmas cycle and the Easter cycle. The latter is very much larger than the former, occupying more than three quarters of the year. (You can see in the illustration two black lines where these two liturgical seasons or cycles join.)

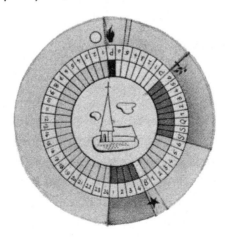

Each of the two liturgical cycles is divided in a similar manner into three parts: first, a preparatory section (colored in violet, the penitential color). Secondly, the feast itself (in white). And finally a third section which is, as it were, a prolongation of the feast (in green). Thus we get Advent and Lent corresponding; similarly Christmastide and Eastertide; while the After-Epiphany-period corresponds to the time After-Pentecost in the Easter cycle.

It is interesting to notice—and we should point it out to the children—that one of the liturgical cycles is concerned with our Lord as an infant; the other—the Easter cycle—has to do with His life as an adult. A similar division will be revealed to the children themselves, as they put out the Time Line of our Lord's life; for this shows the same two divisions (with the unique exception of the Finding in the Temple).

Having put together the complete circle, the child then puts out the little labels representing the subdivisions—Advent, Christmas, etc., as shown. He places a picture of our Lord in the center of the circle, to indicate that the liturgical year revolves round "The Sun of Justice." He puts down the arrow to indicate the direction in which time is moving. And at the top of each circle are placed two labels indicating the two different kinds of years.

Second Material: The Sundays and
Chief Feast Days of the Year.

Having understood that there are thus two kinds of years, both of which will go on repeating themselves until the end of the world—and having learned the main seasons in each of them, and their respective orders—the children can now go on to make a study of the Sundays and feast days in the liturgical year, and the particular liturgical periods in which they occur.

For this we need a much larger circle—perhaps two feet or thirty inches in diameter. This is divided into the same six divisions as the material for the liturgical year already shown. But there is now this difference: the whole circumference of the circle is divided into fifty-two equal sections, which correspond to the fifty-two Sundays in the year. Corresponding little slips of labels are made, one for each Sunday in the year. These are shaped like the examples given below.

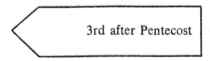

Other important feasts are also included, such as Christmas, Easter Sunday, Pentecost, Corpus Christi, the Assumption of the Blessed Virgin Mary, and also Ash Wednesday and Good Friday. When a feast comes *during the week* a little circle is placed on the line that separates the Sunday *before it and the Sunday following.* And the name-slip is made to point to the feast in question as below.

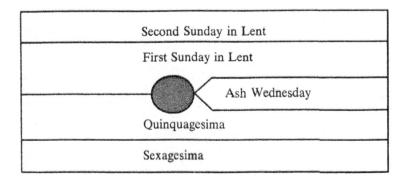

The name-slips are all kept together in a box; and the exercise consists in taking any one at random, and finding its place on the corresponding segment on the circumference of the large circle. In the accompanying illustrations you see two children at work at this exercise. In one picture they are just starting; and in the other—taken about a quarter of an hour later—they are nearing its completion.

The larger circle represents the liturgical year with its 52 Sundays. The smaller circles represent the solar and liturgical years with their seasons. The correct names are written on slips and placed on their corresponding positions. In the center of the circle on the left is a golden sun; in the center of the other is a picture of "the Sun of Justice."

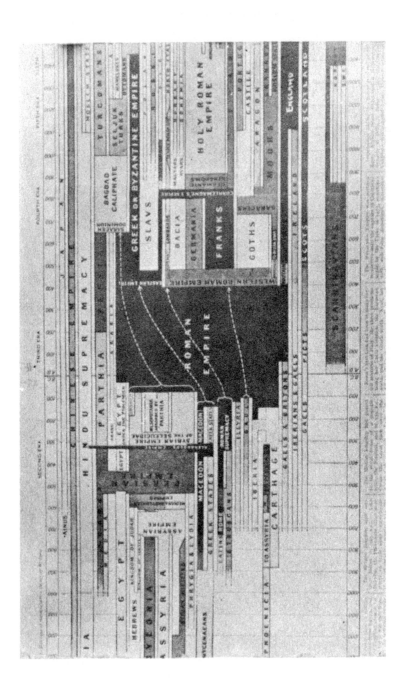

240

CHAPTER FOURTEEN

CHURCH HISTORY AND GEOGRAPHY

O ne of the most valuable principles which is to be found working again and again in the Montessori System is what one might call the principle of rising above one's knowledge, and by doing so seeing something new, and often quite unexpected. What happens is this: in some form or another, we take the knowledge we already have and spread it out in two dimensions. And then we look down upon it, so spread out, from above: by doing so we discover something new. This happens on various intellectual levels in the Montessori System—in fact, it also occurs even on the sensorial plane. One could give endless examples. The exercise known as "Odds and Evens" is a good one; for when the child has spread out the knowledge of number that he already knows, in a special way suddenly he sees that there are two kinds of numbers—odd and even. A similar thing happens in *"The Bird's-eye view of the Decimal System"* when he discovers the hierarchy of numbers; or again, later on, in studying the differences between the squares of numbers.

Now look at the History Chart. There the historian has put down—all spread out on one page—what he knows about the life history of the different nations both B.C. and A.D. And what strikes one at once? One sees all the various nations of the ancient world—Egypt, Persia, Greece, Gaul, Iberia, Carthage, Britain—all being swallowed up one after the other by the Roman Empire. You see the Roman Empire as an immense homogeneous solid bloc extending across the then known world, and lasting for some three to four centuries. Then about the year 400 A.D., it breaks up; and once more we see Europe divided into many different nations, some of which have lasted down to the present day.

Show this Time Chart to any intelligent person, be he Christian, pagan or atheist, and ask the question: "Where in the history of European civilization (and the Near East) —where do you think some unique and unparalleled event took place?" and he would be bound to point to the period of the Roman Empire. And of course this is literally true. That is the period of history when God Himself, having assumed human nature, came to earth, lived upon it as a mortal like ourselves, just at the time of the Roman Empire—at the beginning of it.

One sees the marvelous working of Divine Providence, because the *Pax Romana* was a perfect setting for the spread of the Gospel. For it must be remembered that, as the proverb says, if "all roads lead to Rome," all roads lead away from it, too. And along those many and splendid roads, secure in the social stability maintained by the Roman governors and army—along those roads many of which are still in existence—the Christian missionaries hurried with their "Good News" to Egypt, Greece, Gaul, Spain, Switzerland, and even to far-off Britain. How wonderful and beyond all human planning are the ways of God!

This idea has been beautifully expressed by Abbot Marmion in his book *Christ and His Mysteries:*

We have marveled at the profound ways of Divine Wisdom in the preparation for the mystery of the coming of the God-Man.

While by a succession of marvels Eternal Wisdom keeps intact among the chosen people the ancient promises, unceasingly confirmed and developed by prophecy, while even the successive captivities of the Jewish people, who at times became unfaithful, once made to serve the spread abroad of the knowledge of these promises even among the nations of the Gentiles, Wisdom likewise directs the destinies of the nations.

You know how, during the long period of several centuries, God, who holds the hearts of kings in His hands, and whose power equals His wisdom, establishes and destroys the most vast empires one after the other. To the empire of Nineveh, reaching as far as Egypt, follows that of Babylon; then, as Isaiah had foretold, God "calls His servant Cyrus (king of Persia)," and places the scepter of Nebuchadnezzar in his hands. After Cyrus He made Alexander the master of the nations until He gives the world's empire to Rome, an empire of which the unity and peace will serve the mysterious designs of the spread of the Gospel.

To show a child of 8 to 12 a chart like this is a good thing; but it would be much better if one could—using the chart as a basis—work out some activity, which would attach the child's concentration upon it for a longer time.

One could, for instance, cut out the Roman Empire in plywood, and have strips or rolls for the separate nations; and in this way build up the chart. First the separate nations of the pre-Christian era would be put down, ending with the Roman Empire; and after the fall of Rome, the nations could begin again, being set down in separate strips.

And, of course, one would explain to the children—at first in a group collectively—how this was a preparation for the coming of our Lord and His teaching. And one could also have a card prepared to go with the material, briefly recapitulating what has already been explained to them.

Time Line

For many years all Montessori schools have made use of an

arithmetic material called the "Thousand Bead Chain." It consists of a chain of one hundred ten-bead bars. The first thing to do with it is to spread it out to its full, and very imposing, length along a corridor or veranda or hall. Having done this, the child then places one hundred-cards at their correct intervals, like stations along a railway line. (That is what the boys are doing in the picture on this page.)

Certain ingenious teachers have discovered that this material could be used, with great effect, to indicate visually the meaning of various important historic events—each bar representing a century. This led to a further development— the making of a special History Time Lines. In these, too, the centuries were marked out; but the scale was changed so as to be able to include a greater span of time than just 1,000 years.

The Time Line shown in this picture begins at 2,000 B.C. and goes on (hopefully!) to the year 2,000 A.D. There is a small golden strip in the middle of it representing the thirty-three years of our Lord's life; and the crucifix has been placed, very prominently, at the end of it. Children using this apparatus become accustomed from their earliest years to the fact that our Lord's Coming is the central fact of all human history.

Many and varied are the activities connected with the Time Line, both in secular and religious history. Take the history of the Jews, for instance, up to the time of the Messiah. A special material has been made to illustrate this. It begins with the patriarch Abraham and—passing down through Joseph, Moses, the Judges, Kings and Prophets, etc., ends with St. Anne and St. Joachim and our Lady. The activity consists in placing pictures with names, dates, and descriptive "captions" at their proper places on the B.C. Time Line from 2000 B.C. (Moses) to Herod, the Star of Bethlehem and the Blessed Virgin Mary.

To children working with this Time Line one does not need to stress these things. They protrude by themselves, and are brought home to the children as they work, which is of course all the better—for as Froebel said: "Even a quarter of a truth, discovered by a child for himself, is of more value to him than the whole of it coming secondhand from another person."

Here someone has had another brain wave. Six pictures representing the "Six Days of Creation" has been put down before the Time Line commences and resulting in the Creation of the world—visibly represented by the globe. This brings in the idea that God was at the very beginning of history, as well as visiting it (in the Incarnation) in the middle of it.

It is beyond question that children who have gained their religious knowledge through such a vital method would be less likely to lose interest in the subject when they leave school. Vital education in religion is one of the best ways to prevent that "leakage" which all deplore.

Time Line From 2,000 B.C. to 2,000 A.D.

What You Need
1. A long roll of paper, the heavier the better.
2. Then from an old broom handle, cut two pieces about 18 inches long. To these, the ends of the Time Line are attached, leaving, of course, some blank paper at the end to wrap around the sticks. The Time Line can be rolled and unrolled by means of these sticks, either partially or completely.
3. The centuries should be marked by transverse lines going across the paper at equal distances; five inches is an ideal distance, so that every half-inch represents ten years. These lines marking the centuries should be in one color for B.C., and another color for A.D. They

Moving outdoors in England we see a multiplicity of Time Lines in operation at once. The girl in the foreground is placing miniature statues of famous saints on the cities or districts with which they were connected.

A Time Line representing the Life of Pope Pius XII. The pictures and cards along the line represent the major events in his life before and after his succession to the Throne of Peter.

should be marked transversely, beginning 2,000 B.C., the next 1900 B.C., the next 1800 down to 0. After the year 0 the numbers will, of course, go in the opposite direction, thus 100, 200, 300, etc., up to (if we ever get there!) 2,000 A.D. These dates should also be written in two different colors, one for the B.C. and the other for the A.D. centuries; and the wooden handles should be painted correspondingly.

4. On the small stretch of our Lord's life (0 to 33) there should be a golden strip right across the Time Line; and, when the line is put out a crucifix should be placed next to it to indicate the most important date in all history.

How To Use the Time Line

The general principle for the use of the Time line is that, in some way or other, the events of history which we want to recall are placed on, or next to the Time Line, at their approximate dates. This can be done by preparing labels on slips of cardboard *or* by having pictures of the various events mounted on cards with the date on the back.

One could have just a simple Time Line dealing only with the history of the Jewish people in the B.C. part, or a more complicated one which includes also the great events in secular history, such as the fall of Nineveh or the Battle of Marathon or Alexander the Great or Julius Caesar's campaign, etc.

The Centuries A.D.

I suggest in the A.D. centuries one could put in the names of the great saints like the apostles, St. Ignatius of Antioch, St. Augustine, St. Benedict, and so forth. One could also include on different colored labels the Councils of the Church, finishing off with Vatican II.

The Distribution of Cardinals

I recently came across a newspaper article headlined "The Red Hat Covers the World." One could make a very good material out of this in the following manner:

1. One would have a large map of the world about the size of a Montessori rug with the names of the countries in it.
2. You could have the necessary number of little labels with red hats on them and the name of the country on the other side.
3. The exercise will consist in putting out the little labels (and pictures of the red hat) on their respective countries.

The Hierarchy

One could have a separate material dealing with the respective degrees in the Church hierarchy, from the pope at the top to the parish priest at the bottom.

The Authority of the Church

The Church's authority is unique in the manner in which it came into existence, unique in its nature and function, unique also in its *modus operandi*. It is vitally important that children should gain a clear understanding of the nature of this authority and a willing obedience to "The Living Voice" of the Church, as expressed through the papacy. It should be made abundantly clear to them that the authority of the Church is a continuation of the divine and absolute authority of Christ, whose contemporaries observed that "He spoke with authority and not as the Scribes and the Pharisees."

They should also be made to realize how this same divine authority was delegated to, and vested in, the primacy of St.

A Time Line of Pope John XXIII

Peter and the apostolic college; and how it has been passed on down the centuries. By the use of a specially prepared Time Line, the more advanced can study at what periods in history the Councils were brought into action and the special problems and crises with which they had to deal. In this way the children will be able to envisage Vatican II in its true historic perspective, and at the same time—through this understanding—become more ready to willingly obey any further pronouncements on faith and morals which may in due course emanate from Rome. For, as Goethe once put it, we can only give an authority our willing obedience if we respect and believe in it.

Even young children can gain some idea of what is meant by "The Power of the Word" and the operation of a delegated authority, if the matter is presented to them in a vivid and dramatic way by means of anecdotes, or through little scenes which they can act out among themselves. For example, they can appreciate how the word of a king can pardon the life of a condemned man through his authentic messenger; or how the tremendous power of a great nation is vested in the word of its ambassador, and with that word can "let slip the dogs of war."

Such an approach to the subject will help children to understand the special significance of the word "sent" as used by St Paul in his letter to the Romans (10, 15): "How can they preach unless they be 'sent'?" Or again when the apostle says, "We are Christ's ambassadors and God appeals to you through us" (2 Corinthians 5, 20) they will realize that this is more than a mere figure of speech, for the apostles and their modern successors are veritable ambassadors of a real kingdom—the kingdom of heaven on earth—a truth signified by the fact that the very word "apostle" means "one sent."

The miniature oratory of St. Anthony's School, London.

BIBLICAL GEOGRAPHY

In dealing with Biblical Geography we use the same method, i.e., always with an individual activity, freely chosen by the child, and carried on as long as he wishes, and, as always, there must be that necessary concomitant of freedom—the "Control of Error."

(1) *The Jigsaw Map.* This is a very useful device, but in making it, we must remember that the different parts of the jigsaw (which have to be put together) must be significant in themselves. We must not, therefore, just cut into small pieces at random without reference to what each piece stands for. Thus if we make a jigsaw map of Palestine at the time of our Lord, we should divide the map up into the historical divisions found at that epoch—Judea, Samaria, Galilee and so on, with also a part of the Mediterranean, the Lake of Galilee and the Dead Sea.

For the *Control of Error* we should have a key map, which would list the names of the provinces, the various seas and lakes, and any other names we wish to include. Then, after the child has put the pieces together, he can place the names on the provinces and also on the different towns, mountains, etc. If the map is made of plywood, we could have a small hole made where there is a town to be named. The names could be fixed on those little pins that caterers use for labeling the different kinds of sandwiches, etc., on a table, like this:

The sharp ends can be clipped off with plyers and then the pin inserted in the corresponding hole. *Or* it could be just as well managed by little flat labels with one end cut to a point which can be placed next to the dot representing the city or mountain, etc. It is not, of course, essential to have a jigsaw map. The same method can be used with any map. What one needs always: a) the key map, b) the blank map— with dots for the towns to be named, and c) a little box or envelope with the labels, prepared to be placed on the blank map.

The Wandering of the Children of Israel

It would be a good thing, too, to have a large map made illustrating the *Flight of the Jews from Egypt* (the Passover), their passage of the Red Sea, their wanderings in the desert, Mount Sinai, and so on until they come to the Promised Land. One could have the names of the important places and also little corresponding cards, telling briefly what happened at each place, e.g., the Ten Commandments and Mt. Sinai, the place where Moses struck the rock, etc.

The Traveling Church

Another thing which interests children is the story of how Moses, under the direction of God, caused the children of Israel to build THE TABERNACLE, which was in effect a

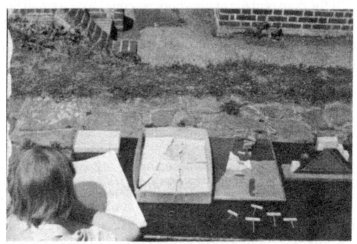

Two maps of Palestine in the time of our Lord. The one on the right is a jigsaw map, each segment representing a different district (e.g., Samaria). When the map has been successfully put together the names of towns, rivers, lakes and other places mentioned in the Gospels are inserted with name-tags on pins. At first the child does all this with the aid of the control map, left. But after a while she will only use it to correct any mistakes she might have made.

Traveling Church. There is an excellent account of this in *The Illustrated Bible History* (B. Herder) chapter 38. It also gives a very good illustration of the Tabernacle. I once had a man make a model of the whole thing—which was an immense success. It was placed on a large area of plywood (covered with sand which was glued on) and the whole thing could be taken apart (as could the original) when it was time to move on, i.e., when the pillar of smoke moved away from the Holy of Holies.

One should also have models or, at least, pictures of the Large Altar with Ramp, the Bowl for Ablutions in the area; and also of objects kept in the Holy of Holies and in the Tabernacle.

The Map of Jerusalem

A most valuable material is the *Map of Jerusalem and its Environs.* One could put the walls of Jerusalem in plastic, or something more permanent; and one could have small movable models of Herod's palace, Pilate's residence and of the houses of Annas and Caiaphas, as well as the Temple.

One could have little movable labels of the various places of interest on the map, e.g., Gethsemani, Bethany, Calvary, the Damascus Gate, etc.

Best of all, of course, would be to make a model of the district showing the hills and valleys.

Later on, this could be followed up with a model of Solomon's Temple which was stationary, and did not need to "move on." Still later, one could show how there is a tabernacle in the Catholic church, an altar for sacrifice, and other parallels.

HISTORY AND GEOGRAPHY COMBINED

Another useful exercise which combines geography and history is as follows:

A Plan of Jerusalem. All important sites, the Temple, Pilate's Palace, the house of the Last Supper, etc. are put in place. (Rome.)

Detail from the model of the Temple used at the Montessori Centre, Rennes, France, and described in Chapter Eleven.

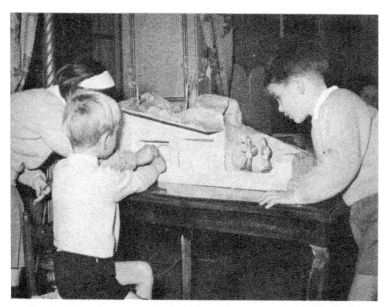

A model of the Tomb from the Cavalletti School in Rome. Notice the inner chamber, stone at opening, soldiers on guard.

On a map of the world this child is placing pictures of missionary saints like St. Francis Xavier, and also the places in which various missionary orders are especially active.

On a map of Europe a girl is placing pictures of saints who are especially identified with cities or districts—e.g., St. Martin of Tours, St. Francis of Assisi, St. Patrick, etc.

Here the sites of our Lady's apparitions are identified with appropriate pictures or images—Montserrat, Lourdes, Guadalupe, Fatima, etc.

Geographical Details of Our Lords Life

SET I.

1. Jesus was born at _____ in _____
2. To escape the fury of Herod the Holy Family fled from _____ to _____
3. After their return from the Holy Family settled at _____
4. Missed by His parents Jesus was found, as a boy of 12, in the Temple at _____
5. Jesus was baptized in the river _____
6. Jesus was tempted by the devil in the desert near _____
7. Jesus worked His first miracle at _____ in _____
8. Jesus spoke to the woman of _____ at Jacob's well at _____
9. _____Jesus raised the widow's son to life at
10. _____Jesus caused the miraculous draught of fishes in the Lake of _____

SET II.

1. St. Peter was the first to confess our Lord as the Son of God at_____
2. Zacchaeus, the publican, climbed in the sycamore tree to see Jesus at_____
3. Jesus often stayed with His friends, Mary, Martha and Lazarus, at the village of _____ near _____
4. Jesus sent the devils out of the madman into the herd of swine at _____ on the eastern shore of Lake____
5. In the parable the man "who fell among thieves" was going from _____ to _____
6. Jesus made the city of _____ on the Lake of

_____His center when living in Galilee.

7. Jesus cured the blind man (Bartimeus) as He entered the city of _____

8. Jesus suffered His agony in the Garden of _____

9. Jesus was crucified at a place called _____ just outside the city of _____

10. After His Resurrection Jesus walked with two of His disciples who were going to _____ a village eight miles from _____

11. After His Resurrection Jesus made a fire and cooked breakfast for His disciples on the shore of the _____

12. According to tradition Jesus ascended into heaven after having blessed His disciples at Mount _____

The names used in this material are written on little cardboard slips in duplicate. There must be two sets of names—one set to be inserted in the blank spaces on the card with the writing on it; and the other set to be placed on the corresponding points on the blank map.

At first the children will do it with repeated references to the keys (a) the written sentences with no blanks, and (b) the key map. But soon they will learn to do it without consulting the keys.

BIBLICAL ANIMALS

Montessori suggests that it would be a good thing to have some sort of material for the children dealing with the various animals which are mentioned in the Old and the New Testament. There should be a picture of the animals and a card, covered with cellophane, on which there is a short story about the animal in question. These should be kept together in a box and the exercise would consist in placing on the table the cards with the animals on them, and then after reading the story, placing the card next to the animal to which it corresponds.

Note on Method

With the smaller children these animal stories will have to be: (1) First of all told to them collectively and, (2) Written out, preferably in script writing, in a very simple form, each story on a separate card. (3) Pictures or models of the animals could all be kept in a little box, or a series of boxes, not more than ten stories in each; and the corresponding cards could be kept either in or next to the box of animals. The children can then put out the animals on their table in a line. Then take a story, read it and place it next to the animal in question. It is quite likely that the children might wish to make their own little book, by copying the stories themselves and placing a drawing or a tracing of the animal on the opposite page.

Old Testament Animals

1. *The plagues of Egypt.* These supply us with a number of creatures such as the frogs, the swarm of flies, the locusts.
2. While the children of Israel were in the desert we might

mention (1) the *quail* that God sent in great quantities for food and, (2) the story of the Golden Calf.

3. *Jonah and the whale.* This is a most dramatic story and children love it; they like to write it out and illustrate it themselves.

4. *Elijah and the raven.*

5. *The lion.* (1) Samson's riddle to the Philistines, "Out of the strong came sweetness." (2) The young David, a shepherd boy, kills a lion and a bear. (3) Peter says that the devil like a roaring lion goes about seeking whom he can devour.

6. *The impertinent boys, the prophet and the bear.* This is the story of the impudent boys who made fun of the prophet Elisha in the woods, calling out: "Go up, thou baldhead." Whereupon two bears came out of the forest and destroyed them—this was their punishment.

New Testament Animals

1. *The donkey.* (1) Used in the flight to Egypt, (2) Palm Sunday procession into Jerusalem.

2. *The mother hen.* This comes in the story when our Lord, on turning around the corner suddenly saw Jerusalem spread out before Him and His disciples; then He burst into tears and exclaimed, "Jerusalem, Jerusalem, that slayeth the prophets! How often would I have gathered thy children together as a hen gathers her young under her wings, but thou wouldst not."

3. *Sheep.* There are many references to sheep and our Lord as a *Good Shepherd.* The parable of the Good Shepherd and the lost sheep could be prepared for a little action with a model fold and the number of sheep. Similarly we could have the hireling shepherd who flees when

the wolf comes and devours the sheep. There are many other references to sheep and shepherds.

4. *Dogs.* (1) Mentioned by the Canaanite woman, (2) the poor Lazarus outside the rich man's house and the dogs that came and licked his sores.

5. *Pigs or swine.* (1) Prodigal son became a swineherd and even ate their food. (2) The herd of swine that became possessed by devils and rushed down the cliff into the sea and drowned. (3) "Neither cast your pearls before swine, or they will trample them under their feet and turn and tear you."

6. *Fish.* There are many references to fish in the New Testament. (1) St. Peter and the miraculous draught of fishes ("Do not be afraid; henceforth thou shalt catch men"). (2) The money for the Temple tax found in the fish's mouth (Matthew 17, 26).

7. *Camel.* "It is easier for a camel to pass through the eye of a needle, than for a rich man to enter the kingdom of heaven."

An exercise in matching objects with their correct identifying slips. Instead of the usual "Farm" this girl is using a crib and the attendant animals. Later she will construct phrases and sentences out of the reading slips.

EPILOGUE

FUTURE DEVELOPMENTS

The Montessori principles, taken collectively, can be compared to the leaven in the Gospel "which a woman took and put in three measures of meal until it leavened the whole batch." In the same way the Montessori "leaven" is working in the sphere of education, raising it to a higher level. Thus, in the course of the half-century which has elapsed since the Montessori movement began, it has worked its way into the teaching of many new subjects, such as history, geography, biology and physical science—and the process is still going on.

This has also been the case in the teaching of religion. Those who have read this book will have become aware, in some degree, of how the Montessori "leaven" has been working actively and independently in different countries, through the practical researches of Montessori teachers in England, France, Rome and other places. In fact, so much research has been carried out in this field that, when it came to the final preparations for this second edition of the *Child and the Church*, it was realized that there was more material on hand than could be conveniently included in one volume.

As a consequence of all this new development, certain chapters, which were included in the original book, had to give way *pro tern,* in order to permit the inclusion of other matter which was deemed more urgent, though not necessarily more important in the long run. For this reason certain aspects of the subject have had to be postponed for another volume, which is already more than halfway to completion.

This new book will include a long chapter by Montessori—*La Vita in Cristo (Life in Christ)*—which is an explanation of the liturgical year. Along with this will be found illustrated suggestions for the construction and use of teaching materials dealing with the various aspects of the liturgical year and the major feasts.

There will also be three other chapters by Montessori, which were included in the original edition, bearing on the psychology and practice of her Method. The first, *Child Character,* portrays the beneficial effects upon the child's character which appear after he has lived for some time in the "Prepared Environment," under the wise guidance of a Montessori directress. Among these can be mentioned the ability to concentrate, a love of order, the capacity to choose the occupations he needs for his further development, the acquisition of a *willing* obedience which is the result of a new self-mastery, a serene and joyous disposition, and a remarkable self-discipline.

In another chapter, on *Sensitive Periods,* Montessori gives a brilliant account of her doctrine of special creative periods in the child's development, with practical suggestions as to how they should be made use of in education. In a third chapter, *Advice to Directresses,* the *Dottoressa*—drawing on her long experience—indicates the immense importance of the attention by the directress to certain apparently insignificant details, which are, however, really matters of supreme practical value in the successful running of a Montessori class.

As it is possible that some of the readers of this book may not have had the opportunity of making themselves acquainted with the underlying psychological principles of the Montessori Method, the next book will also contain the chapter on *The Main Principles of the Montessori Method*, which was in the first edition. There will also be a chapter on *The Montessori Method in Relation to Moral Training*. This is concerned with such questions as the following: "If the child, under the Montessori System, is permitted to choose his work—and enjoys doing it—will not this be a bad preparation for the inevitable drudgery that he will have to face later on in life?" In another chapter, *Such is the Kingdom*, the editor points out the striking parallel which exists between the characteristics and manner of life carried on by "normalized" children, in the Montessori Prepared Environment, and the characteristics and life of Religious in convent or monastery.

The second part of this forthcoming book deals—as in Part Three of the present volume—with the practical aspects of the teaching of religion according to Montessori Principles. Of special interest is the account of her *"Missalle dei Bambini"* or Children's Missal. In creating this Montessori has displayed her deep knowledge of child psychology, combined with her customary originality in catering to his needs. Thus, for example, the Propers of the Mass are not kept in the Missal itself and the child has to prepare his Missal beforehand by finding them and inserting them in their right places. This self-activity involves, on the part of the child, some knowledge of the liturgical seasons, and also of the structure of the Mass.

Incidentally, Dr. Montessori had some original ideas as to how we might introduce the Ten Commandments to quite young children. Some of her followers—in particular the Franciscan Sisters at their school in Mill Hill, London—have devised an excellent material which, by its very nature, obliges the children using it to make continual meditations on the scope of the several commandments and their bearing on their daily life in school and at home. This also will be described, with particulars as to how to use it.

The Teaching of the Sacraments, both in general and in particular, will also be considered in the forthcoming book. Montessori used to point out that, in connection with many of the sacraments—five to be exact—there is some form of promise to be made; and she was of the opinion that greater emphasis should be made on the seriousness of the promises involved. It is hoped that, by the time the next volume is out, the Marchesa Cavalletti's excellent materials for teaching the sacraments of baptism and confirmation, already published in Italy (at the *Centro Catechistico Paolino in Rome)* will be obtainable in an English translation.

In the *Constitution on the Liturgy,* recently issued by the Ecumenical Council, *sacramentals* are mentioned as part of the liturgy of the Church. By sacramentals are meant "certain pious practices or objects blessed by the Church" *(Catholic Dictionary).* Some of these are included in public worship—such as the making of the sign of the cross, the *Asperges* at the beginning of the principal Mass, the ashes placed on the forehead on Ash Wednesday, the kissing of various objects (such as the crucifix on Good Friday), processions such as those of Corpus Christi and other occasions; the lighting of candles from the Paschal candle; the use of incense, and many other such rites. Even such simple actions as standing up at the Gospel, kneeling at the Consecration, or genuflecting before the tabernacle are sacramentals, and serve to increase the devotion of the faithful. Others are of a more private nature, such as the wearing of blessed scapulars and medals or small relics, the use of a blessed rosary, or the setting up of a crib at Christmastime.

Sacramentals as a whole have a special appeal to young children whose attention is most easily obtained through a "sensory-motor activity." We have seen, as Montessori points out in an earlier chapter, how it is a real act of the intelligence for a three or four-year-old to distinguish between dipping one's fingers into water to cleanse them, and doing a similar action in the holy water font prior to blessing oneself; or between the lighting of a candle, for the purpose of illumination, and lighting it for the Holy Saturday ceremony. At a later stage children are thrilled to learn that the sign of the cross was used, in times of persecution, as a secret sign by which the Christians could recognize each other as belonging to the same organization—just as Juniors invent special signs known only to members of their own special group or "gang." At the same age, too, they have a special penchant for signs and symbols—witness the various badges the Scouts wear to indicate they have passed certain tests.

There are many other ceremonies carried out by the Church of a sacramental order which would be of great interest to children if they only had a chance to see them. The rite of the consecration of the bells that are to be used to summon the faithful to church is one of these. It interests and surprises them to learn that each bell is specially blessed and given its own name—just as they were given a name at baptism. In fact, in former times the ceremony was known as "The Baptism of the Bells." In the atrium there would be a special scope for the study of the many various sacramentals used by the Church, and many opportunities for putting them into practice.

Acquainted from the very beginning with the many sacramentals by which the Church hallows even the most ordinary things of everyday life—such as the rooms in his house, his own pets, the family car, his new rosary—the child will grow up accustomed to the idea of the blending together of the natural and the supernatural in one common, dedicated life.

APPENDIX

THE CO-ORDINATION OF CATHOLIC MONTESSORI ACTIVITIES

The Catholic Montessori Guild in England has been inactive for some years chiefly due to the circumstance that most of those who were active in propagating it have recently gone to live in the United States of America. But there is no doubt that it will revive again in some form or other. It is of the nature of things that Catholics in any country, who have become interested in Montessori principles, will seek to apply them to the most important subject of all—the teaching of religion. In point of fact this work has been, and is still going on, independently, in various countries—as will be gathered from Chapters Nine to Eleven in this book. And the same thing is happening in Germany. A few years ago an article appeared in the Osservatore Romano (Jan. 8, 1962) stating that a Montessori Union for Catholic Education had been started under the presidency of Dr. Helen Helming, who has for many years been prominent in the Montessori Movement in Germany. The Union was formed by the united efforts of Catholic parents and teachers of all grades.

The aim of the Union is to make known the principles and methods of the great Catholic educator, Maria Montessori, in Catholic circles, and to apply them in institutions of all kinds. It will collaborate with the Association Internationale Montessori and with the German Montessori Society which has been in existence some years. The renewed interest in the Montessori System—after the Second World War—began in 1953, and was followed up by the publication of various books by Montessori published by the firm of Klett, Stoccarda. There has been a favorable response to this Montessori work among Catholics who have decided to extend the sphere of the application of Montessori principles in their educational organizations.

Pending a more complete and international organization for Catholic Montessori work, we would suggest that if any group of Catholics form themselves into an organization along the lines of the Catholic Montessori Guild (see below) it would be a good thing if they would report their existence, with an account of their activities, to some central point of focus. In the British Isles we would suggest that they communicate with the Rev. Principal of the Montessori Training Center, the Dominican Convent, Sion Hill, Blackrock, Dublin; and in the U.S.A. with Miss Elizabeth Stephenson, who directs an annual Training Course for Montessori Teachers at the Montessori Institute, 2700 28th St., Washington, D.C. In this way the various Catholic activities could be coordinated, leading to the holding of periodical conferences at which specialists could lecture and the various researches going on in different centers collated and developed into an organized body of experience and knowledge.

AIM OF THE CATHOLIC MONTESSORI GUILD

The aim of the Catholic Montessori Guild is to study and apply—under the authority of the Church—the educational principles of Maria Montessori to religious training and development.

In this way children would be enabled, at each stage of their development, to take their fullest share in the life of the Church. Dr. Montessori was convinced that children, from birth, are susceptible to religious influences through their "Absorbent Mind" and through their sensory impressions, long before the age of reason. "It is," she says, "among the simple people, whose women take their children to church while they are still breast-fed that the staunchest faith is to be found."

A special feature, therefore, of the C.M.G. work is to emphasize the importance of surrounding children with the right kind of religious influences during those formative years when children are still too young to take part in formal catechism lessons. To this problem Dr. Montessori applied her profound insight into the soul of the child, with telling and original effect, in methods which are as yet little known. The work of Dr. Montessori for religious education is not confined to the infant stage. She has also made valuable research into the needs of older children and of adolescents. It is one of the aims of the C.M.G. to develop this part of her work.

The application of the Montessori principles to general education leads to the development of many characteristics —such as love of order, intellectual concentration, mutual help and self-discipline—which are not usually associated with children.

These natural virtues should be highly valued because, as St. Thomas tells us, the fullest development of the natural faculties is the best preparation for the supernatural life—in accordance with the principle that "Grace builds upon nature, not destroying but perfecting it."

INDEX